CONTENTS

Rajmohan Gandhi is a biographer, historian and former Rajya Sabha member who has been championing Hindu–Muslim understanding for over sixty years. He has served on university campuses in India, including IIT Gandhinagar and IIT Bombay, and in the US, where he taught at the University of Illinois at Urbana-Champaign from 1997 to 2022. He has authored over a dozen books, including highly acclaimed biographies of Mahatma Gandhi, Khan Abdul Ghaffar Khan, C. Rajagopalachari and Sardar Vallabhbhai Patel. His *Rajaji: A Life* received the Sahitya Akademi Award in 2002.

FRATERNITY

Constitutional Norm and Human Need

Rajmohan Gandhi

SPEAKING
TIGER

SPEAKING TIGER BOOKS LLP
125A, Ground Floor, Shahpur Jat, near Asiad Village,
New Delhi 110049

First published by Speaking Tiger Books 2024

ISBN: 978-93-5447-698-3
eISBN: 978-93-5447-699-0

10 9 8 7 6 5 4 3 2 1

Typeset in Garamond Premier Pro by SŪRYA, New Delhi
Printed at HT Media Ltd, Greater Noida

Introduction

Harsh Mander

This is the second in a series of short volumes that we hope to offer to the Indian people to help foster a better understanding and appreciation of the Indian Constitution, especially in a time when its core values are so contested.

It is fitting that this volume is written by a person who bears the legacy of the freedom struggle, being the grandson on the one hand of Mahatma Gandhi and on the other of C. Rajagopalachari, free India's first Governor General after Lord Mountbatten. Rajmohan Gandhi in his own right is a leading public intellectual, biographer, historian, social and political activist.

It is fitting, moreover, that the first thematic volume in this series is on Fraternity. Fraternity in English means brotherhood. This must of course include sisterhood as well. The Hindi version of the Constitution uses the beautiful word *bandhuta*. Derived from Sanskrit, this means the idea that we are bound to and with each other. Looking at it in another way, *bandhu* means friend, so bandhuta can also be understood as an ideology of friendship.

Fraternity or bandhuta encompasses the lustrous idea that we might have between us enormous differences—of wealth, gender, caste, religion, language, ability, the colour of our skins, the size of our eyes and noses, who we choose to love and marry, the food we eat, the clothes we wear, and so much else—but are *bound to and with each other* despite that. We are brothers, sisters, friends.

Bandhuta is therefore the single most precious idea of the Constitution, but also the hardest to accomplish. So many people teach us hate—our leaders, our peers, our elders, our heroes from films and sports, our friends. We need instead teachers, leaders, philosophers, writers, film-makers, singers, artists, friends and family who teach us love.

For it is not a country founded on hate, fear, division and inequality which we, the people of India promised to build. The country we gave to ourselves was a humane and equal country founded on love. Bandhuta is what brings us together as one country. We are not one country because we are alike. We are one country because, despite every difference in the way we look, eat, dress, speak, worship, love and think, we belong to and with each other. If there are shackles on your feet, I feel my freedom has been stolen.

If you sleep hungry, I am unable to sleep. If your suffer loss and pain, tears well up in my eyes.

India's Struggle for Freedom

Mahatma Gandhi returned to India from the distant shores of South Africa in 1915. He was forty-five years old. The India he returned to, not unlike the one he had left as a young man, was mired in many unfreedoms, the primary one for a great many being political, enslaved as India was to rulers from across the seas for nearly two lightless centuries.

The colonial government could throw for years into prison people who rallied or fought against their rule. Some were hung from the gallows like the heroic young revolutionary, Bhagat Singh, some were banished for lifetimes to the distant Andaman Islands. Even those committed to peaceful, non-violent resistance to foreign rule were beaten back and often bundled into jail, sometimes for long periods of time.

The British colonized India because, at the time they arrived, this was one of the wealthiest and most industrialized countries in the world. In the two centuries of their rule, most industries had been destroyed, farming starved through rack-renting and artisans impoverished. There was misery and hunger in the famine-ravished countryside. The average lifespan of a common Indian was as low as 21 years at the time when Gandhiji returned to India.

The Indian people endured the agony of painful bondage in ways similar to the people of many countries in Asia, Africa and Latin America. A handful of Western countries had carved out large chunks of the globe, rich in natural resources. They devised various systems for arrogating the resources of these countries to their own ends: cotton for their mills, tea for their trade, land for their *lagaan*, food for their granaries, markets for their produce and soldiers for their wars.

The proud people of these enslaved countries, including India, rose heroically in revolt. All struggling people found their own pathways to freedom. What marks out our freedom struggle from most others was that the mainstream of our struggle was founded on the pivotal moral idea of *ahimsa*, or non-violence. Ahimsa means the resolve that I will fight you for my freedom and dignity, resolutely, accepting whatever consequences this battle will extract from me, including a bullet or banishment to prison; but even as I struggle against you for what is right and just, I will never hate you, and I will wish or cause you no injury or harm.

A Broken, Wounded India

The British eventually bent to the resilience of this struggle. However, they left not one but two nations—India and Pakistan. In frenzied riots on both sides of the new border which now suddenly separated sister from sister and brother from brother, a madness of hate seized the sub-continent. Hindus, Muslims and Sikhs slaughtered each other with a viciousness that cast a very dark and long shadow on the celebrations of freedom. Estimates of mortality range up to two million; an uncounted number were raped and abducted. Fourteen million people were cruelly uprooted from their homes, travelling often on foot, weary and heartbroken, for hundreds of kilometres, with their small children and the few belongings that they had been able to salvage on their aching backs. There is only one other distress migration, which humankind has witnessed in the course of recorded history, that was larger than this one. This was the forced trafficking of Africans as slaves to the Americas.

Pakistan was created as an independent nation for the Muslim people who lived in the west and east flanks of the teeming country. Its leaders urged Muslims in other parts of India to move to Pakistan to make this new nation their home.

There were some who advocated that India should be a country *only* for the Hindus—a Hindu India, a mirror image of a Muslim Pakistan. This would be a fitting reply to Pakistan, they felt, and would secure justice to India's overwhelming Hindu majority.

But Gandhiji had led our freedom struggle on the

shining promise that India would be a country where people of every religion (or no religion!), caste, language and gender would be equal citizens in every way. Jawaharlal Nehru, India's first prime minister, declared that India would belong equally to all those who chose to make this their home, irrespective of their religion or community. One of Gandhi's closest associates, Maulana Azad, often spoke glowingly of his great pride, sense of ownership and resolute belonging to this country which he so loved. He declared that he was Muslim *and* he was Indian, and both these identities were inseparable from him, that he was willing to give up neither of these. He said India had given a great deal to its Muslim people, and the Muslim people too had given a great deal to their country. On 23 October 1947, as the country was reeling under the Partition, he stood tall on the ramparts of the grand Jama Masjid in Delhi and made a historic, heartfelt appeal to Muslims living in various parts of India to stay on, because this was their country and would always be.

This call was echoed over and over again by a Gandhi devastated to his soul by the tumult of religious hate and violence in India and Pakistan. He entreated Muslims over and over again to stay on in an India that he pledged would belong equally, in every way, to its Muslim citizens. A very large number of Muslims heeded his call, and the call of Maulana Azad and Jawaharlal Nehru, opting for multi-faith India over Muslim Pakistan.

When India was celebrating freedom in August 1947, however, Mahatma Gandhi was not in Delhi to celebrate as the Union Jack was lowered and the Indian Tricolour raised. He was instead in Calcutta, where Muslims and Hindus were killing each other in what appeared to be an unending bloodbath of hate. He went on an epic fast refusing to eat a morsel of food until the last of the violence had ended. He returned then to Delhi, trying to quell the hate and violence of hundreds of thousands of angry and sullen refugees separated forever from their homeland in what was now Pakistan. (These included my own extended family, uprooted from their birthplace.) He had planned then to travel (pointedly without a visa) into Pakistan to try to douse the fires of hatred that raged in this newly born country. But this was not to be.

Every day, Mahatma Gandhi would hold a prayer meeting, in which he recited prayers from all major religions. One of his favourite hymns included the line: '*Ishwar-Allah tero naam*'. On a winter evening on 30 January 1948, on his way to his prayer meeting, he was killed by a man violently opposed to his idea of an India which would belong equally to all people of all faiths. A stricken people mourned the death of the father of the nation, a man who paved the path to building a country which was humane and inclusive, which assured equal rights as citizens to people of every religion, caste, language and gender.

Babasaheb Ambedkar, who would lead the writing of India's constitution, had warned that any attempt to restrict India to people of the majority Hindu faith would be a 'calamity' for the nation and for democracy.

As the bullets of Gandhi's assassin signalled, not everyone shared this vision for India.

The Constitution—a Dream, a Vision, a Set of Promises

Having shaken off the shackles of two hundred years of slavery in 1947, the Indian people chose to draw up the blueprint of the kind of country free India would be. Unlike several other countries that had newly gained independence around the time, India did adopt wholly or partly a constitution left behind by the departing colonizer. The Indian people resolved proudly that they would write their own destiny, and they did so with solemn and searching reflection and debate for several years.

At the time of India's freedom, the world was still rebuilding and healing from the devastation and wounds left by the Second World War. The Holocaust had left around six million Jews, two-thirds of the entire Jewish people in Europe, dead, many in gas chambers built in Nazi Germany, the state led by Adolf Hitler from 1933 to 1945; along with multitudes of Roma and Sinti people, homosexual men, persons with disability and prisoners of war. The people of the world were learning from this horrific and tragic genocide the dangers of what happens in a country if minorities—religious, racial, ethnic, caste, sexual—are not protected. They were learning the cataclysmic consequences of the politics of hate and division. These were also lessons for the Indian people. The same lessons came out of the horrific Partition riots, and from India's epic freedom struggle.

The centuries of colonial bondage had reduced India from one of the wealthiest to one of the poorest countries of the world, in which famine, illiteracy, sickness and want stalked the countryside. For millennia, the cruel system of caste had made life a living hell for those unfortunate enough to be born into disadvantaged castes. Women were denied rights to property, education, work and dignity, and even sometimes life itself.

Would we change all of this, and how? Who would this country belong to? Who would govern this country? How would the rulers be chosen? What powers would these rulers have? What powers and rights would the people have? And would the country's minorities—religious, caste, tribal and gender—be protected?

It was answers to questions like these that were written into the Constitution of newly independent India.

What is a constitution? It is a dream, a vision, a set of promises; a compendium of guarantees, a store-house of aspirations. It is a solemn articulation of the values that the country will hold close to its collective soul in its journey in the decades and centuries which lie ahead. It is the collective imagination of the destination which the country pledges to reach.

Most constitutions, except for those in the United Kingdom, Israel, Saudi Arabia and a few others, are written documents. The Constitution of India was written by a collective, the Constituent Assembly. They sat in the grand historic circular building which became for over seven decades the Parliament of the Indian republic. The Constituent Assembly had over three hundred members. These women and men were, in a sense, the founding mothers and fathers of the Constitution. They were drawn from the people elected into the provincial assemblies of the time. And about a third were nominated, to ensure that those in attendance included people of every religion, caste, gender, culture, community and profession. The Constituent Assembly did not have members only from the Congress party which led India to freedom; members were invited even from parties strongly opposed to the Congress. One example is Babasaheb Bhimrao Ambedkar, who was the brave, charismatic and inspiring leader of the Scheduled Castes Federation, who had often stood in stout opposition to the Congress led by Gandhiji. Members of the Hindu Right were also invited to sit in the Constituent Assembly. There were many small kingdoms which were merged into the Indian nation, and their representatives were also members of this assembly.

Looking back today, we realize that it should have had many more women, more persons with disability, more Adivasi and Dalit people, many more working poor people, from factories and farms, and more gender minorities. But there's no denying the fact that the fine women and men who sat on the benches of the Constituent Assembly did indeed speak for all the people of India.

The first sittings of the Constituent Assembly began even before India became free, in the winter of 1946. The assembly deliberated for three years. A smaller group was carved out of the assembly called the Drafting Committee, which worked on the detailed draft of the constitution, and each of the sections of this draft were discussed in the assembly and then put to vote.

The chairperson of this drafting committee was one of the most learned men in the assembly, Dr Ambedkar, affectionately called Babasaheb. He contributed invaluably to many of the progressive measures written into our constitution. He was born into a very poor family of a soldier in the Indian army, from one of the most oppressed castes. On people from these castes for centuries was inflicted the most cruel form of discrimination which we know as untouchability. (Shamefully, that and many such practices endure in free India.) The country is fortunate that such a man—highly educated, wise and one who knew from personal experience the suffering of the most oppressed of our people—led the process of writing the constitution. The two women members of the Drafting Committee, Hansa Mehta and Rajkumari Amrit Kaur, contributed spiritedly and thoughtfully to the deliberations, seeking to make the Constitution also reflect the aspirations of the forgotten and oppressed half of the population, women. We owe a lot to the founding mothers and fathers of the constitution, who drew with us and for us the contours of the dream and the promise of a country based on equality and humanity which we resolved to build, one day.

From Mahatma Gandhi, we imbibed the idea and practice of radical love. From Babasaheb Ambedkar we learned the idea and practice of radical equality. These together became the cornerstones of our Constitution.

Hum Log: We, the People of India

Who indeed gave to us our constitution? The opening lines of the document answer this question. They tell us that 'We, the people of India' ('*Hum, Bharat ke log*') gave to ourselves this constitution. Who are 'we, the people of India'? We are the people who lived in this great and ancient land in past centuries; we are the people who were alive in India when the Constitution was framed; and we are the people of generations which followed and are still to follow. 'We' includes our grandparents and parents, it includes each of us who reside in this vast terrain today. And 'we' will include our children and their children one day.

The 'we' in 'we, the people' is the ocean in which many, many different little streams and mighty rivers meet. We derive strength and vitality from the plurality of our magnificent heritage. This kaleidoscope of our diversity is mirrored in our ever-changing natural features—from the Himalayas to the rivers, the forests to the deserts, the deltas to the plateaus, the coastlines to the islands. This kaleidoscope is made up of our music, of our art, of our dance forms, of our *gharanas* of classical music, and of their vibrant intermingling fusions. Of the spectacular range of our culinary choices, our varied taste buds that create a plethora of platters and cuisines, changing every few hundred miles. Of every festival of every religion and culture, which in our land becomes an Indian festival. Of our thousands of dialects and languages, such that if two people are selected at random from any ten in our country, chances are that they will speak different tongues.

India is the glorious symphony of our many different voices. It is a wondrous palette in which you can find every colour in the world, and we are privileged to be able to draw paintings of our lives from this multitude of colours.

All of these, all and every one of us, you and I, make 'we, the people'.

The Preamble

The soul of the Constitution, its essence, is contained in a single page, which is called the Preamble. Every religion has a holy book, and prayer. Some people say that for the people of India, our holy book is our Constitution, and our prayer the Preamble.

But holy books are often placed on an unreachable pedestal; holy books cannot be questioned or changed. The Constitution is not that kind of holy book. It is a book which belongs to we, the people of India, one that protects and guides us through difficult times, but one that can be discussed, challenged and also collectively changed. It is a book of the people, not of the gods. It contains within it the values that the people of India pledge to uphold as the nation is built and as later generations come and go.

The Preamble talks of the kind of country India will be. India will be sovereign, it says. This means its destiny will no longer be controlled by any foreign power. It will be democratic. This means its government will be chosen by its people. It will be a republic, which means that the ruler will not be born into power, in the way kings and queens have been born for centuries. Nor will the ruler snatch power through the bloodshed and brute force of military conquest or coups. The ruler will have to be elected by the people. Anyone, including those born into the greatest disadvantage, will have the right to aspire to become rulers, and seek the support of the people for the right to rule them.

An important question arose before the Constituent Assembly about which people should have the right to vote for their government. India became the first of the newly independent countries to give *every* person—man, woman or transgender, rich or poor, educated or uneducated—exactly equal political power to choose their rulers. One person, one vote. The richest and the most powerful man in the country would have the same single vote as the poorest, most destitute trans woman. A young person born in India today may think this is the most normal thing to do, but it wasn't at the time. It was a brave and radical—and some would say audacious—idea. In Western democracies, for a long time only white men of wealth enjoyed the right to vote. Women had to fight long for an equal right to vote. In the United States of America, for instance, women got the right to vote only in 1920, and African Americans only in 1965. In Australia, aboriginal Australians did not get the right to vote until 1962. In India, the idea of universal suffrage for every person was adopted without any noteworthy dissent.

Many people had feared that Indians were not ready for this radical system of voting rights for all people, called universal adult franchise. Less than one in five people were even literate at the time of Independence; among women there were less than one in ten. But our founding mothers and fathers still resolved to place their faith in the ordinary Indian, even those denied education, wealth and social standing. They ensured that they would be guaranteed as their birth-right the opportunity to participate equally with every other Indian, the most wealthy, educated, socially or politically powerful, in choosing their governments, and through this, in building the nation and their collective destinies. For a society that would not allow the 'lower' castes to step inside schools and temples, to possess land, and to live with dignity; for a society that would not allow some women even the chance to be born, let alone to own and inherit property and to work shoulder to shoulder with men—for this society to resolve to ensure the same and equal right to vote for every person, though not the end of the road, was a truly iridescent beginning to the great adventure of building a new nation.

From the first election in India in 1951, people from around the world watched with wonder and admiration as impoverished people, disadvantaged castes and women formed the longest lines outside polling booths. This has remained unchanged even until today. India's people of disadvantage are found to choose carefully and thoughtfully. The wonderment is that the people democracy has most let down are those who continue to have the greatest faith in this same democracy.

The Preamble goes on to mandate that the country will be socialist. This means many things. That the government must be committed to ensuring a decent standard of living for all its citizens. It must protect them from hunger and joblessness, and ensure equal and affordable education, health care, housing, decent work and social protection to all. It means a conscious state resolve to prevent the concentration of wealth in a few hands.

The Preamble also lays down that India will be a secular country. This means that the government will have no religion, and it will neither practise nor promote any particular religion. It will not discriminate in any way between people on the basis of their religion, whether they form a tiny minority of people, numbering not more than a few hundred people, following their traditional faith, or those who follow the religion of the largest majority of the Indian people. It also means that the state will promote harmony and goodwill between people with different belief systems.

In a particularly significant judgement of the Delhi High Court which decriminalized homosexuality in 2006, despite the stout opposition of people of almost every religious faith in the country, the bench declared that India's secular constitution gives every citizen of the country the freedom to follow their faith and beliefs. Of course, if their moral rules contradict the morality of the Constitution, it is constitutional morality that must prevail over individual religious beliefs. This ruling was first overturned by the Supreme Court, and then restored, but sexual minorities are still denied the equal right of people of the same sex to marry.

The Constitution promises equal justice to all people, in all aspects of their lives. Justice here does not simply mean what goes on in the courts. It means fairness. It means that people will not face discrimination in society because of their religion, caste, gender, sexuality or disability. They will not face discrimination in their participation in the economy, in work and in the markets. Women and men (and gay and trans people) will have equal access to employment, based only on their merit and not their gender, and will get equal pay for equal work. The ancient system of *begar*, or forced labour, imposed mostly on the most disadvantaged castes was abolished by the Constitution. No one could be kept as a bonded labourer. All persons are also to be treated fairly in their political life, when they go out to vote, to campaign, or to fight elections.

One of the most important promises of the Constitution is of liberty, or freedom. In many protests around the country, slogans are raised for *azaadi*. Azaadi means liberty or freedom. What kinds of freedom or azaadi does the Constitution guarantee? It mandates freedom of thought, expression and belief. This means that every citizen is free to think, speak and believe in ideas which may not conform to the views of the government in power, or of the majority of people. In other words, it grants the freedom of conscience, the freedom to dissent, to disagree with power—political, social and economic power. Many believe that this freedom lies at the core of democracy.

The right to dissent must also carry the freedom from fear, the assurance that I will not be punished for holding beliefs different from those of the powerful. Rabindranath Tagore speaks glowingly of such a country, in which 'the mind is without fear, and the head is held high...' History stands witness that it was only when brave women and men raised their voices against established orthodoxies of their time—when Galileo said the world was round and not flat, or when Savitribai Phule and Fatima Sheikh established schools for girls when the kitchen was believed to be the only fitting confine for women, when Raja Ram Mohan Roy railed against a woman being burnt on her husband's pyre for *sati* or children being tied in marriage, when Babasaheb Ambedkar fought the idea and practice of caste in which the accident of your birth determines all your life chances, condemning you to a life of humiliation and discrimination, barring you from education and dignified work—that the world became a better place for later generations. We are here today because they refused to conform. Conformity leads to deadwood and regression. The freedom of conscience, the freedom to dissent, is therefore central to the pledge of liberty for all, which our constitution guarantees.

The Constitution also importantly assures the freedom of faith and worship. It protects the right of every person to follow her religion, her forms of worship, her ways of life including her choice of food and clothes. It allows people not just to follow but also to propagate their faith, and to establish their religious institutions.

There are other vital freedoms as well which are mandated by our constitution. These include the freedom to pursue the occupation we choose, to move to any part of the country and to form associations or unions, to write and produce art, poetry, novels, books, philosophy, theatre, films—and video games and Instagram videos—which reflect our belief systems and our creativity.

There are many ways that we are not equal. Some of us run faster than others, some cook better, some sing or dance or paint better, some score better marks in class, some can become mothers and others cannot, and so on. But above all of these differences, the Constitution recognizes us all to be equal in a fundamental way: we are equal in human dignity and human worth. There is, from this yardstick, no difference between the wealthiest person and someone begging for alms outside a temple or dargah. It is because of this inherent intrinsic equality that we all have an equal vote and equal rights and freedoms.

The Constitution requires that the government should ensure equality of opportunity. This means that wherever you might be born, in a village, a slum, the city streets or a mansion, you are entitled to the same opportunities to study, in the same quality school or college, and the same chances to develop your potential, whether for intellectual pursuit, sports, music, art or anything else. It also requires governments to ensure equality of status. This is an even more difficult task. It means that at least to some degree, governments must ensure more equal conditions of life to those who are more disadvantaged. This can only be done by what is called redistribution, by taxing the wealthy to ensure the right to a decent life to the disadvantaged; and by reservations or affirmative action, which recognizes that people who have for centuries been treated unequally need special support in education and jobs for them to achieve real equality in the conditions of their lives.

The Constitution also firmly and categorically bans the practice of untouchability. This—along with the principle of one person, one vote—are arguably the most radical sections of the Constitution. It outlaws unambiguously a practice that has brutalized and shamed Indian society for at least two millennia. Untouchability is one of the most troubling, cruel and disgraceful parts of India's historical legacy. By the accident of birth into a particular caste, it condemns people to a life where they are not allowed into religious shrines, share food or water with other people who will avoid so much as their touch, and will prevent them from walking on the same road as them or riding a horse in a wedding procession, or studying in school or college. The Constitution prohibited these shameful practices. This provision transforms the Constitution, at least in part, into a luminous moral document, seeking to confront and atone for the crimes of our history.

After, justice, liberty and equality, the fourth, and in many ways the central, pillar of the Preamble is fraternity, which is the subject of this volume.

Dr Ambedkar rightly said that the most important idea in the Constitution is the idea of fraternity. It is this idea which affirms the equal dignity of every individual. We learn from him that the other foundational ideas of the Constitution can be conceivably accomplished even if there is no fraternity. But this would be possible only by enforcing these through the strong arm of the state. However, if there is fraternity in society, then you don't need the state to enforce justice, liberty, equality: instead, these become the natural order of things.

Our Reality

But what is our reality? Look around. It is apparent that 'we, the people of India' have built a country still far distant from the India we promised ourselves in our constitution. And in some ways this distance is only growing.

Think of which of the magnificent and solemn pledges that we made to ourselves have been realized. What has become of the dreams of our founding mothers and fathers?

A great deal has indeed been accomplished. Every person in this country continues to hold the power to choose her government. Citizens of a large majority of newly independent countries were denied or lost this power, to military coups and dictators. Fewer people in our country are poor, fewer sleep hungry than when we won our freedom. The average length of life has risen from 37 years in 1947 to 67 years three quarters of a century later. We have some fine institutions for teaching the humanities, engineering, medicine and management, our warehouses are overloaded with food grains, we are the IT back office of the world, and our cities glitter with gated colonies, luxury cars and crowded malls.

But look carefully, and you will find that one in every third child is still malnourished. This means that their bodies and brains are not allowed to develop to full potential for lack of nutritious food and clean water. Children of the poor study in separate, significantly less resourced schools than children of the rich. Many are not allowed to study at all, and instead parents still feel compelled to send them out to hard labour. Every second woman is anaemic. Eight out of ten doctors in India work for for-profit private hospitals, and government spending on health care in India is among the lowest in the world. If poor people fall ill, they cannot rely on good quality publicly provisioned health care. Wealth accumulates in an incredibly small numbers of hands, and this is barely taxed. At the other far end of the spectrum, nine out of ten workers toil in casual, insecure, unsafe jobs at dirt wages. As they age, most have barely enough pensions to secure their aging with dignity and health care.

People still suffer horrible violence and discrimination because of their religion, caste and gender; or because they walk the paths of equality that is their right; or when they choose to love and marry outside the socially prescribed boundaries of religion, caste and gender. Adivasis are dispossessed by large powerful corporations from their forests and homelands, and are branded as Maoists and jailed when they protest. Crowds gather and lynch Muslim and Dalit men, beating them to death, and proudly videograph these crimes and circulate these on social media. Untouchability continues with pitiless and ferocious violence. Dalits are beaten and killed in India even today for growing a moustache, for building a two-storied house, for asking for fair wages, for just advancing in life through their own hard work and talent; their children thrashed for drinking water from an earthen pot meant for their 'high-caste' teacher. And these horrific crimes are rarely punished.

Governments punish instead people who disagree with them. The freedom to dissent is dying, with fear and official targeting choking voices of truth. The freedom of religious faith is threatened by the politics of majoritarian hate. People spend years in prison because they are too poor to afford legal counsel, because the courts are clogged and uncaring, because they belong to stigmatized religious and caste identities, or simply because they dare to challenge the injustices of the state.

Reflect on the essence, the morality, the soul of our constitution. It is not perfect. With the hindsight of history, there are some things we might want to change. But contained in it are the iridescent dreams we had for this nation when it threw off its chains of slavery. These are the ambitions, the lofty and worthy goals that we, the people set for our country. And since these are promises which we have made unto ourselves, it is for you and I, 'we, the people of India', to rebuild this country into the kind, equal, free and just land imagined by our founding mothers and fathers.

We must build with the bricks of our hearts and minds, of our dreams and our struggles, of our accomplishments and our sacrifices, and I hope, of love.

This Series

India recently celebrated seventy-five years of its Independence. As one small tribute to the Indian freedom struggle, we propose a series of ten books that summarize in simple, accessible language the core values, imagination and pledges of the Constitution. The themes for these books we have been drawn mainly from the Preamble—Secularism, Socialism, Democracy, Justice, Liberty, Equality, Fraternity. In addition, we include the themes Scientific Temper and Federalism; these too are essential to the morality of the Indian Constitution. We are fortunate that the fine minds and hearts who we approached—some senior, some younger—all agreed generously to contribute to this series.

These books draw from the Constituent Assembly debates, and indeed from those that preceded them. Each book also looks at how these ideas evolved in independent India, through court rulings and executive actions. The series also looks at the relevance of these ideas to the challenges of the India of today, the extent to which the state, the polity, the economy and society remain faithful to these ideas, the principal contestations to these ideas, and finally, the ways in which these ideas are important for India's future as a humane, democratic state.

Dr Neera Chandhoke, one of India's leading political scientists, and Distinguished Fellow of the Centre for Equity Studies, consented to help me bring out the series and has also written the opening book for it. Ravi Singh, co-founder of Speaking Tiger and one of India's finest editors, agreed to publish this series. We hope to get these translated into Hindi and other Indian languages as well.

At a time when the morality and pledges of the Constitution are under assault, it is our fervent wish that this small project—an effort to unpack and popularize it—will be useful as resistance, defence and public affirmation of the luminous morality of the founding document of India.

'Can you, every one of you, lay your hand on your heart and say that every sufferer, whether Hindu, Sikh or Muslim, is your own brother or sister?'

—Gandhi in Delhi on Diwali day, 12 November 1947
(*Collected Works*, vol. 90, p. 18)

Author's Preface

That I should write this short book was someone else's idea, but I wrote it willingly, even enthusiastically. For the plan to provide 'in simple accessible language' the 'core values, imagination and pledges of the Constitution', including fraternity, made total and immediate sense.

When, at the end of 1949, our Constitution was adopted, its contents surprised and impressed the world. In the years that followed, the world seemed to marvel that India, so diverse in language, caste and religion, was adhering to the spirit of our Constitution. For a long time, no community felt deliberately excluded from the nation's steady advance on multiple fronts.

Now, however, influential voices inside and outside India sharply question the virtues of liberty, equality and fraternity. Much, though not all, of the questioning remains indirect, for an open advocacy of coercion, inequality or hate causes embarrassment even in today's rough world.

Whether expressed openly or not, the urge to coerce, diminish or even demonize some sections of the population is now palpable within India and beyond. Hence this little book.

The story of every precious jewel in our Constitution must be heard. I am fortunate to have a chance to summarize and present the wonderful story of fraternity. Thank you, Harsh Mander and your multi-generational team, for giving me the opportunity.

And thank you, Speaking Tiger.

Rajmohan Gandhi
12 December 2023

Chapter I

We Belong to One Another. Or Do We?

It was holiday time in the year 1901. Sitting with an older brother and a cousin on a train that had left Satara, nine-year-old Bhimrao Ambedkar was excited. His father, Ramji Sakpal, an army cashier at the time, had asked the youngsters, who were living with Sakpal's sister in Satara town, to join him in the village where he was working at the time, Koregaon, which lay near the railway station of Masur, both located within the large Satara district of what at the time was Bombay Presidency, later to become Maharashtra.

As a result, the boys had their first rail experience. Wearing—as Ambedkar would put it—'new shirts of English make, bright bejewelled caps, new shoes, and new silk-bordered dhoties', they had arrived at Satara station, where, for the first time in their lives, 'they sipped lemonade'.

The train ride was great fun, and at Masur, where they got off, the stationmaster was inclined at first to be friendly, assuming from their clothes that these were high-caste boys. The instant he found them to be Mahars, the stationmaster turned cold.

Ramji Sakpal was not at the station—he hadn't known when the boys would be arriving. Masur's bullock-cart drivers refused to take the untouchable boys to their destination, but finally, as night fell, one cart-owner said the *boys* could drive his cart, for double the fee, while he, the owner-driver, would not sit in the cart and only walk alongside. He didn't wish to be polluted by the boys. Desperate to reach their father/uncle, the boys accepted the cruel offer.

The slow, bumpy ride took an entire night. No one along the way was willing to help the boys find water. Finally, 'famished and demoralized', they arrived where their father was. Previous to this experience, Bhim had faced his share of discrimination. Among other things, he had become used to sitting in a corner in his Satara schoolroom, separated from the rest of the class. A 'touchable' boy had to open a tap for Bhim to get water to drink. Yet the bullock-cart ride from Masur was a fresh and sudden escalation of indignity.[1]

Much later, in April 1921, Mohandas Gandhi would recall a time in Rajkot, Gujarat, which was about twenty years prior to the train and cart journey in western Maharashtra that Ambedkar could never forget. 'I was hardly yet twelve,'

Gandhi would say, suggesting that he was speaking of the year 1881, 'when this idea [that untouchability was a curse] dawned on me'.

'A scavenger named Uka, an untouchable,' Gandhi continued, 'used to attend our house for cleaning latrines. Often I would ask my mother why I was forbidden to touch him. If I accidentally touched Uka, I was asked to perform the ablutions, and though I obeyed, it was not without smilingly protesting. I was a dutiful and obedient child but had tussles with them on this matter. I told my mother that she was entirely wrong in considering physical contact with Uka as sinful.

'While at school I would often happen to touch the "untouchables", and as I never would conceal the fact from my parents, my mother would tell me that the shortest cut to purification after the unholy touch was to cancel the touch by touching any Mussulman passing by.'[2]

A second polluting touch would cancel the first contamination.

~

How men treated women was not less important to Ambedkar or Gandhi than questions of caste or religion. Ambedkar's empathy across the gender divide leaps up from the dedication page of his farsighted 1941 volume, *Pakistan or the Partition of India*. There Ambedkar wrote that he was inscribing the book 'to the memory of Ramu'—his wife Ramabai, who had died in 1935—'as a token of my appreciation of her goodness of heart, her nobility of mind and her purity of character and also for the cool fortitude and readiness to suffer along with me which she showed in those friendless days of want and worries which fell to our lot'.

As for Gandhi's attitude to women, it was highlighted by, among others, Nirmal Kumar Bose, the anthropology professor who assisted Gandhi as a translator in riot-torn Noakhali during the 1946–47 winter, before Noakhali became part of East Pakistan (the future Bangladesh). Noakhali had seen rapes and forced conversions in the 1946 autumn, and Gandhi had gone there to instil courage in victims and repentance in aggressors.

Reporting that much of Gandhi's time in Noakhali was spent with Hindu women stricken with fear, Bose wrote of Gandhi's 'daily ministrations on behalf of love' and 'the extreme tenderness with which he regarded each individual' relating woes to him.[3] More than consolation, however, it was fortitude, it seems, that Gandhi sought to inject. Bose observed that in the course of one meeting with bereaved women, 'Gandhiji's face hardened, and he said that they must recover their courage'.[4]

Not forgetting the curse of untouchability, to caste Hindu women in Chandipur in Noakhali, Gandhi proposed (on 3 January 1947) another difficult step: they should invite a Dalit 'every day to dine with you'. Or at least ask him 'to touch the food or the water before you consume it. Do penance for your sins.'[5]

The seventeen months between August 1946 and January 1948 saw many moments of agony in the geographical space that was India at the time but became India and Pakistan in August 1947. Communal killings began in Kolkata on 16 August 1946 and spread thereafter to Noakhali in September–October 1946, to Bihar in October–November 1946, to western Uttar Pradesh (then the United Provinces) in November 1946, to the western half of what still was a united Punjab in March 1947, and from July–August 1947, in a terrifying crescendo, to both halves of now divided Punjab.

Yet on 15 August 1947 India became independent. Ecstasy!

In his final months, as gifted lieutenants moved from recent prison terms to bastions of power and privilege, Gandhi vacated his invisible throne of influence over the nation's best-known leaders and walked as a peacemaker on India's troubled ground. To knit Indians together, he walked—or, at times, travelled by boat, road or train—in Bengal, Bihar, Delhi and what today is Haryana's Mewat region. He also wrote, spoke, prayed and fasted.

His message was that we belong to one another. If 'they'

kill one of 'our' children, 'we', said Gandhi, should adopt one of 'their' children and raise them in 'their' faith. The message seemed tough. Yet it accorded with the human conscience, and noble individuals were applying it on their own. On 2 November 1947, during that season of madness, Gandhi spoke publicly of his happiness on learning of a Muslim in Lahore who was sheltering a Sikh friend.

Friendship, then, was the answer to hate, to turmoil! About three months later, when an assassinated Gandhi joined the roll of hate's victims, the lesson sank in. Goodwill returned. The tide of madness dissipated.

A democratic republic was soon launched. Steered by Ambedkar, the Constitution was created. Equal protection, irrespective of caste, creed or gender, was pledged. To a fair extent, it was also demonstrated. Seeing Indian democracy in action, the world of the 1950s and 1960s marvelled.

~

Each time we look at it, the Preamble to our Constitution seems to say something fresh to us:

> WE, THE PEOPLE OF INDIA, having solemnly resolved to constitute India into a SOVEREIGN SOCIALIST SECULAR DEMOCRATIC REPUBLIC and to secure to all its citizens:
>
> JUSTICE, social, economic and political; LIBERTY of thought, expression, belief, faith and worship;

> EQUALITY of status and of opportunity;
>
> And to promote among them all FRATERNITY assuring the dignity of the individual and the unity and integrity of the Nation;
>
> IN OUR CONSTITUENT ASSEMBLY this twenty-sixth day of November, 1949, do HEREBY ADOPT, ENACT AND GIVE TO OURSELVES THIS CONSTITUTION.

As far as fraternity is concerned, we may mark right away that the Preamble highlights its connection first to the citizen's dignity, and next, immediately thereafter in fact, to the nation's unity and integrity. In the precise words of a short half-sentence, the Preamble underscores fraternity's significance to us and our fellow citizens as independent, self-respecting individuals—and, simultaneously, as interdependent citizens who respect one another, strengthen one another, and fortify the nation.

This half sentence is a powerful illumination, in fact a brilliant and unforgettable illumination, of fraternity. The pages that follow will dwell further on fraternity's meaning to us as Indians, on why and how it entered our Preamble, on how it entered the world's politics and laws, and on other aspects of fraternity. But at this outset it is necessary to recognize the word's limitations.

The biggest weakness has to do with the word's maleness. If fraternity is to be privileged, isn't half of humanity being excluded right away? Doesn't fraternity assault equality? This is not just a twenty-first-century question. Even in the eighteenth century, when *liberte, egalite et fraternite* first resounded in their country, French women protested at their seeming exclusion.

To this question there are two answers, neither of them entirely satisfactory. One is that the apparent maleness here is merely superficial. What the word summons, and what it has broadly been understood to summon, in India and elsewhere, is the regard that human beings without exception deserve from one another. Thus, a common chant of India's freedom movement, *Hindu–Muslim Bhai-Bhai*, was widely assumed to include *Behen-Behen* and *Behen-Bhai*.

The other answer is that alternative single-word expressions for the intended warmth are yet to acquire widespread acceptance.

Goodwill, friendship, empathy, solidarity, harmony, compassion, respect and bonding are wonderful words each of them, each in a different way, and there are other similar expressions, but perhaps none will be widely accepted today as a superior substitute for fraternity. The Hindi/Hindustani words *bandhuta*, *maitri* and *dosti* also possess profound strength, but not all in India speak Hindi.

Moreover, whatever word we use in conversation with fellow citizens as an alternative to fraternity, the fact remains that the Preamble has chiselled that particular word into our minds, including the minds of Supreme Court judges. Thus, rejecting a petition for a commission for renaming all roads and places bearing the names of 'foreign invaders', Justices K.M. Joseph and B.V. Nagarathna pronounced as follows on 27 February 2023:

'The golden principle of fraternity is of the greatest importance and rightfully finds its place in the Preamble. It means that harmony alone will lead to the togetherness of the country.'[6]

While conceding freely that fraternity is an imperfect word, we can also recognize, apart from its wide usage, that what it connotes is an essential quality. When using the word, and recognizing that the Preamble uses it, we can focus not on its alphabet, but on its historical and widely accepted broader meaning—in the world and especially in India.

Irrespective of gender, caste, religion, language, ethnicity, blood, region or whatever else, all Indians belong to one another. Or should. We are kin to one another, related to one another. We feel, or ought to feel, one another's joys and one another's pain. That's fraternity.

As was revealed by the two stories with which we began, imbibing and preserving fraternity will remain a challenge. On 25 November 1949, the day before our Constitution was finally and formally passed, here is what Dr Ambedkar told the Constituent Assembly:

What does fraternity mean? Fraternity means a sense of common brotherhood of all Indians—of Indians being one people. It is the principle which gives unity and solidarity to social life... Without fraternity, equality and liberty will be no deeper than coats of paint.

Chapter II

Fraternity and the US and French Constitutions

Though in many eyes a new or recent nation, the United States of America possesses the world's oldest written constitution. Its preamble was composed, along with the rest of that constitution, in 1787. Usually attributed to a Pennsylvanian called Gouverneur Morris, the preamble reads as follows:

> We the People of the United States, in order to form a more perfect Union, establish Justice, insure domestic Tranquility, provide for the common defence, promote the general Welfare, and secure the Blessings of Liberty to ourselves and our Posterity, do ordain and establish this Constitution for the United States of America.

In 1791, i.e. four years after the American constitution was adopted, the First Amendment laid down that liberty of faith or religion, freedom of speech or of the press, or the right to assemble and speak out, could not be abridged:

> Congress shall make no law respecting an establishment of religion, or prohibiting the free exercise thereof; or abridging the freedom of speech, or of the press; or the right of the people peaceably to assemble, and to petition the Government for a redress of grievances.

If liberty was emphatically asserted here, neither equality nor fraternity was brought up as an essential norm. It took many decades and a massive civil war, fought from 1861 to 1865, for the enslavement of America's Blacks to be declared unlawful. Passed in 1865, the Thirteenth Amendment read:

> Neither slavery nor involuntary servitude, except as a punishment for crime whereof the party shall have been duly convicted, shall exist within the United States, or any place subject to their jurisdiction.

Five years later, in 1870, the Fifteenth Amendment seemed to guarantee that *every* American adult would have the right to vote:

> The right of citizens of the United States to vote shall not be denied or abridged by the United States or by any State on account of race, color, or previous condition.

That 'every American' only meant 'every American male' was, however, well understood. America's women waited for their right to vote all the way until 1920. That year's Amendment, number 19 in a series that extends as of date to number 27, reads:

> The right of citizens of the United States to vote shall not be denied or abridged by the United States or by any State on account of sex.

If we take the American preamble along with amendments 1, 13, 15 and 19, we observe a clear and early commitment to liberty, and a slowly but steadily growing constitutional embrace of equality. But what about fraternity? Some might detect a faint trace of that value in the preamble's phrase 'domestic tranquility', an even fainter one in its words about promoting 'the general welfare', and a concealed or potential presence in the phrase 'a more perfect union'.

In July 1776—eleven years *before* the American constitution was framed—the Declaration of Independence (at first described as a 'team' draft but in fact the handiwork, we are told, of Thomas Jefferson, who would become the third US president) also spelt out norms for the large country in the Western Hemisphere that was about to wage a revolutionary war to end its subjection to 'mother' England.

> 'We hold these truths to be self-evident', the Declaration stated, 'that all men are created equal, that they are endowed by their Creator with certain unalienable

> Rights, that among these are Life, Liberty and the pursuit of Happiness.—That to secure these rights, Governments are instituted among Men, deriving their just powers from the consent of the governed,—That whenever any Form of Government becomes destructive of these ends, it is the Right of the People to alter or to abolish it, and to institute new Government, laying its foundation on such principles and organizing its powers in such form, as to them shall seem most likely to [a]ffect their Safety and Happiness.'

'All men are created equal.' 'Men only?' the future would ask. With all its weakness, however, the Declaration's affirmation of equality, made well before the constitution was written, was historic, and would make new history.

~

While the chief purpose of these pages is to look at fraternity and enquire into its significance as a constitutional and social value in India, including by comparing the Indian story with changes elsewhere, some historical concurrences are worth marking. The final decades of the eighteenth century, when *Americans* fought to throw off *British rule*, was also the stage when the *French* fought to throw off *feudalism* with a revolution in their own country.

That end-eighteenth-century period saw other noteworthy happenings. For one thing, the French openly assisted the bid in America to oust the British. During that period, moreover, the English and the French warred with each other on Indian soil for possessing India, and the two European powers struck alliances with regional Indian rulers to reach their goal.

It was a time when winds and sails rather than steam or oil propelled ships. Still, British and French military officers moved across the wide seas (and lands) that lay between America and India. Cornwallis, an army officer in America on the losing British side, became Governor-General of India. In 1791 and 1792, Cornwallis led two massive campaigns to subdue Mysore's Tipu, who was tenaciously defying British expansion in South India.

While Hyderabad's nizam and the Marathas, with their headquarters in Pune, backed Cornwallis, the French supported Tipu, who repulsed Cornwallis's first attack in 1791 but had to accept a humiliating compromise after the Briton's successful thrust in the following year. Two of Tipu's sons, ten and eight in age, were handed over to Cornwallis as hostages, kept under him for two years, and returned only after heavy fines imposed on Tipu had been fully recovered.

We should return, however, to America's Declaration of Independence of 1776, where we saw equality heralded as a norm. Some might claim to detect aspects of fraternity in the words, 'life, liberty, and the pursuit of happiness', which are described as 'unalienable rights' from which, evidently, no Americans may be excluded. However, fraternity as such is certainly not named either in the Declaration or in the US constitution.

On the other hand, Abraham Lincoln's words in his Second Inaugural, delivered on March 4, 1865, seemed to breathe the very essence of fraternity.

> 'With malice toward none,' said Lincoln, 'with charity for all, with firmness in the right as God gives us to see the right, let us strive on to finish the work we are in, to bind up the nation's wounds, to care for him who shall have borne the battle, and for his widow and his orphan—to do all which may achieve and cherish a just and lasting peace among ourselves and with all nations.'

When Lincoln spoke these words, the pro-slavery South was close to defeat after four years of brutal fighting. By the end, five weeks later, of the US's nineteenth-century civil war, that confrontation had taken 620,000 American lives. Even when combined together, the two World Wars of the twentieth century would not extinguish that many American lives.

In 1861, Lincoln had justified the commencement of the civil war by invoking the equality laid down eighty-five years prior to that in the Declaration of Independence. Placed against the background of the harrowing events of the civil war, Lincoln's 1865 call for binding up America's wounds, eschewing ill-will, and remembering '*all* nations', was not merely statesmanlike. It acquired lasting influence.

In the decades that ensued, that call gained quasi-constitutional authority. In spirit if not in words, fraternity had entered the US constitution.

~

Although the core of modern France's constitution formed itself in the last quarter of the eighteenth century, the constitution's text was reformulated in 1958, under the leadership of Charles de Gaulle. The preamble to this 1958 version states that

> The French people solemnly proclaim their attachment to the Rights of Man and the principles of national sovereignty as defined by the *Declaration of 1789*...

Article 1 announces that

> France shall be an indivisible, secular, democratic and social Republic. It shall ensure the equality of all citizens before the law, without distinction of origin, race or religion. It shall respect all beliefs...
>
> Statutes shall promote equal access by women and men to elective offices and posts as well as to positions of professional and social responsibility.

Article 2 declares:

> The language of the Republic shall be French.
>
> The national emblem shall be the blue, white and red tricolour flag.
>
> The national anthem shall be *La Marseillaise*.
>
> The maxim of the Republic shall be 'Liberty, Equality, Fraternity'.
>
> The principle of the Republic shall be government of the people, by the people and for the people.

~

What was France's Declaration of 1789? In August of that year, i.e. just two years after the US adopted its constitution, a National Assembly of France, where a king, Louis XVI, still sat on the throne, adopted a resolution that among other things showed awareness of America's 1776 Declaration of Independence. France's August resolution, or declaration, warrants a patient and even painstaking look, for it contains more than a dozen claims:

> The representatives of the French people, organized as a National Assembly, believing that the ignorance, neglect, or contempt of the rights of man are the sole cause of public calamities and of the corruption of governments, have determined to set forth in a solemn declaration the natural, unalienable, and sacred rights of man...

[T]he National Assembly recognizes and proclaims, in the presence and under the auspices of the Supreme Being, the following rights of man and of the citizen:

1. Men are born and remain free and equal in rights. Social distinctions may be founded only upon the general good.
2. The aim of all political association is the preservation of the natural and imprescriptible [i.e. inherent and innate, not prescribed by an outside authority] rights of man. These rights are liberty, property, security, and resistance to oppression.
3. The principle of all sovereignty resides essentially in the nation. No body nor individual may exercise any authority which does not proceed directly from the nation.
4. Liberty consists in the freedom to do everything which injures no one else; hence the exercise of the natural rights of each man has no limits except those which assure to the other members of the society the enjoyment of the same rights...
5. Law can only prohibit such actions as are hurtful to society. Nothing may be prevented which is not forbidden by law, and no one may be forced to do anything not provided for by law.
6. Law is the expression of the general will. Every citizen has a right to participate personally, or through his representative, in its foundation. It

must be the same for all, whether it protects or punishes. All citizens, being equal in the eyes of the law, are equally eligible to all dignities and to all public positions and occupations, according to their abilities, and without distinction except that of their virtues and talents.

7. No person shall be accused, arrested, or imprisoned except in the cases and according to the forms prescribed by law...
8. The law shall provide for such punishments only as are strictly and obviously necessary, and no one shall suffer punishment except it be legally inflicted in virtue of a law passed and promulgated before the commission of the offense.
9. As all persons are held innocent until they shall have been declared guilty, if arrest shall be deemed indispensable, all harshness not essential to the securing of the prisoner's person shall be severely repressed by law.
10. No one shall be disquieted on account of his opinions, including his religious views, provided their manifestation does not disturb the public order established by law.
11. The free communication of ideas and opinions is one of the most precious of the rights of man. Every citizen may, accordingly, speak, write, and print with freedom, but shall be responsible for such abuses of this freedom as shall be defined by law.

12. The security of the rights of man and of the citizen requires public military forces. These forces are, therefore, established for the good of all and not for the personal advantage of those to whom they shall be intrusted.
13. A common contribution is essential for the maintenance of the public forces and for the cost of administration. This should be equitably distributed among all the citizens in proportion to their means.
14. All the citizens have a right to decide, either personally or by their representatives, as to the necessity of the public contribution; to grant this freely; to know to what uses it is put; and to fix the proportion, the mode of assessment and of collection and the duration of the taxes.
15. Society has the right to require of every public agent an account of his administration.
16. A society in which the observance of the law is not assured, nor the separation of powers defined, has no constitution at all.
17. Since property is an inviolable and sacred right, no one shall be deprived thereof except where public necessity, legally determined, shall clearly demand it, and then only on condition that the owner shall have been previously and equitably indemnified.[7]

Similarities in the American and French declarations or constitutions should not surprise us. When Frenchmen assisted America's War of Independence on American soil, ideas and philosophies were exchanged face to face. Like much of Europe, France was under the spell of the Enlightenment, which French thinkers had helped initiate. If intellectuals such as Rousseau, Voltaire and Montesquieu influenced America's political thinking, American figures like Benjamin Franklin, Thomas Jefferson and Thomas Paine spent consequential periods in France, contributing to its outlook.[8]

Also written into France's constitution, we may note, are these 'principles of the French Republic':

- Social welfare
- Laïcité [the preferred French word for the kind of secularism upheld in France]
- Democracy, ensuring that Parliament and Government are elected by the people; and
- 'Indivisibility', the view that the French people, speaking one language, are united and that all of them are equal.

'Indivisibility' here seems to mean what we want from fraternity and seems very close also to 'solidarity'.

We may note further that from 2005 onwards the French constitution has included ten articles of a Charter for the Environment.

~

The historical realities touched upon by us merit closer attention. The last quarter of the eighteenth century found both the French, as they strove to end feudalism, and the Americans, as they started to free themselves from a distant monarch, underscoring popular sovereignty, separation of powers, the individual's liberty and equality among individuals.

Apart from exporting participants to the American Revolution, the French had also paid some of that Revolution's financial cost. Involvement in America's struggle contributed to France's fierce economic crisis of the 1780s, which had been aggravated by, among other factors, bad harvests, drought, cattle disease, skyrocketing bread prices and extravagant expenditures by King Louis XVI and his wife, Marie Antoinette.

In May 1789, the King asked representatives of France's three 'Estates' (as these were called)—the clergy, the nobility and the commoners—to meet in his Versailles palace to address the crisis. Forming 98 per cent of the population, the third category of 'the commoners' included farmers and farmworkers, most of them with little or no land, artisans, the urban poor, small businessmen and better-off members of the bourgeoisie. It was this third estate that paid all the taxes. The first two categories paid nothing.

Though it was unable to find an immediate solution, the Versailles convention, which was soon converted into a National Assembly, highlighted the regime's bankruptcy and the pointlessness of retaining a king.

In June, representatives of this third estate took an oath on an indoor tennis court in Versailles that they would not disperse until they had framed a constitution for France. On 14 July, to prevent a suspected coup, the Bastille in Paris, France's great prison, was stormed. In August, 'feudalism's death' was proclaimed by the National Assembly, and the Declaration of the Rights of Man, summarized earlier in this chapter, was issued.

Three years thereafter (in 1792), the king, Louis XVI, was seized. On 21 January 1793, he was guillotined. Nine months later, Marie Antoinette met with the same fate. By this time, in June of 1793, the Reign of Terror—when revolutionary insurgents conducted massacres and public executions—had taken place. Thirteen months later, in July 1794, Robespierre, a leader of the French Revolution and, according to some, the first person to have spoken of 'liberty, equality, and fraternity', was executed.

Occurring in 1799, the coup of Napoleon Bonaparte was in some ways the climax of the French Revolution.

While acknowledging the blood spilled in the 1780s and 1790s, the French have to this day proudly retained the *liberte, egalite, fraternite* motto. When, after the Napoleonic era, the 1848 Constitution was drafted, 'Liberty, Equality, Fraternity' remained there as a 'principle' of the Republic.[9]

Asserting this, a modern website of the French foreign office adds: 'Solidarity was sometimes preferred to equality, which implies a levelling of society, and the Christian connotation of fraternity was not accepted by everyone.'

This motto—*liberte, egalite, fraternite*—was inscribed again on the porticos of public buildings on the occasion of the celebration of 14 July 1880 (when, for the first time, Bastille Day was proclaimed as a national holiday). The motto was retained in the later constitutions of 1946 and 1958, which created the Fourth and Fifth French republics. A proud and integral part of France's national heritage, the motto is found on coins and postage stamps used by the general public.[10]

A twenty-first-century European group focusing on human rights, Civil Liberties Union for Europe (Liberties), has this to say about the historical and current meanings of 'liberty, equality and fraternity':

> Liberty, or the right to live freely and without oppression or undue restriction from the authorities, is a core value in a democratic society. So too is equality. This is not only about treating each other as equals, but also that every person is viewed equally under the law.
>
> Fraternity, at its core, is about solidarity—we're all partners in building and maintaining the safe, free and fair society we all want to live in.

> [Historically,] the inclusion of *fraternité* was not without criticism. In response to its inclusion, journalist Olympe de Gouges wrote the Declaration of the Rights of Woman and of the Female Citizen...
>
> [Today] the motto is deeply important to many French people, a source of pride that encapsulates the values of a modern and diverse France. But it means different things to different people. Many still feel that its values of equality, liberty and solidarity apply in their truest form, to all people.
>
> Others, however, especially those of the Rassemblement Nationale and other right-wing movements, apply the motto only to French citizens. They even go so far as to suggest that migrants are being treated even better than citizens, and that citizenship should be harder to attain.[11]

~

What the *liberte, egalite et fraternite* motto also did was to give birth to a *global* belief system that would eventually produce modern-day human rights treaties, including the Universal Declaration of Human Rights (UDHR), which the United Nations passed in 1948. Reproduced below, the language of the mid-twentieth-century UDHR bears unmistakable and easily recognizable traces of the American and French Declarations of the last quarter of the eighteenth century:

> Whereas recognition of the inherent dignity and of the equal and inalienable rights of all members of the human family is the foundation of freedom, justice and peace in the world,
>
> Whereas disregard and contempt for human rights have resulted in barbarous acts which have outraged the conscience of mankind, and the advent of a world in which human beings shall enjoy freedom of speech and belief and freedom from fear and want has been proclaimed as the highest aspiration of the common people...
>
> Now, therefore, the General Assembly proclaims this Universal Declaration of Human Rights as a common standard of achievement for all peoples and all nations...
>
> *Article 1*: All human beings are born free and equal in dignity and rights. They are endowed with reason and conscience and should act towards one another in a spirit of brotherhood.
>
> *Article 2*: Everyone is entitled to all the rights and freedoms set forth in this Declaration, without distinction of any kind, such as race, colour, sex, language, religion, political or other opinion, national or social origin, property, birth or other status...

~

To recognize these American and French precedents for struggles for human rights does not of course mean that similar examples were not offered elsewhere. Nor do the precedents imply that the US and France have been faithful to these principles. It is well known that in both countries an influential stream of politics is today driven by the insistence, whether or not openly articulated, that *only a section of humanity* is worthy of liberty, equality and fraternity.

The people of the U.S. and France have to reflect on the distance between fraternity, on the one hand, and their laws and the enforcement of these laws on the other. How people of colour, indigenous groups, women, immigrants and sexual minorities fare before the police and judges is a question that they have to ask of themselves.

We may mark something else. Popular with sections in France, the notion that in order to possess equal rights those living in their country should yield to what for many is an unpleasant homogenization and refrain, in any public space, from displaying a distinctive religious symbol, seems to conflict with fraternity.

In the next chapter we will return to India and try to figure out—in very broad terms—how human rights have fared or flourished in the climate created by our history and culture.

Chapter III

Democracy and Fraternity in Indian History

It is well known that central characters in the Upanishads (someone like Yajnavalkya, the philosopher, for example) and in the *Mahabharata* (Yudhishthir, the eldest Pandava brother) are subjected to challenging Q and A exercises. Which shows that ancient India was familiar with a crucial aspect of democracy, namely questioning and debate, and to a core ingredient of effective debate, namely persuasive reasoning.

It is also impressive, and a matter of pride for Indians, that those early debaters included brilliant women like Gargi and Maitreyi.

Then there is the magnificent story, also descending to us from the Upanishads, of young Satyakama Jabali. When the boy requested a famous sage to accept him as a disciple, the sage asked for the boy's lineage. Replied Satyakama: 'Sir, I don't know. Once, when I asked my mother about this, she replied, "I used to serve many people and got you in my youth. I don't know your father's name. But you are my son. You are Jabala's son. You are Satyakama Jabali."'

Thrilled by the boy's truthfulness, the guru accepted him as a disciple, even though tradition required him to reject one not indisputably born of a Brahmin father. His mother's son, and bearing her name, Satyakama Jabali ended up as a famous philosopher.

Glimpses of this kind, whether literary, scriptural, or bequeathed by epics, are undoubtedly exciting. For one thing, they confirm that democracy was not invented by the Global North which then taught it to the Global South, a supposedly slow or resisting learner. They do not, however, prove that democracy was practised widely or consistently on the soil of ancient India.

We may nonetheless assume that those glimpses were lodged somewhere in the Indian mind. We may further assume that during succeeding periods at least some Indians may have envisioned a polity where questioning and free speech were encouraged, even if such polities did not thrive around them.

Fraternity, too, was at times portrayed in sections of our ancient texts, perhaps nowhere more powerfully than in the *Ramayana*. In Kamban's twelfth-century Tamil *Ramayana*, for instance, Prince Ram tells Guha, the low-caste boatman who ferries the exiled prince across the Ganga, that he, Guha, was now his *brother* and therefore King Dashrath's 'fifth son', after the well-known four—Ram himself, Lakshman, Bharat and Shatrughna.

Later, in Kamban's retelling, Ram would call the monkey-chieftain Sugriva, too, his brother (as also Dashrath's 'sixth son'), and Ram would speak of Vibhishan (sibling of Ravan, the demon king who had abducted Ram's wife Sita) as another brother and thus Dashrath's 'seventh son'.

Tulsidas, too, in his sixteenth-century *Ramcharitmanas* portrays the deep Ram–Vibhishan bond. While Tulsidas's Ram does not quite call the demon-prince a 'blood-brother', he feelingly addresses Vibhishan as *sakha*, or intimate friend:

> सुनहु सखा कह कृपानिधाना।
> (Listen, friend, said the one who is the abode of grace.)

Along with such portrayals of fraternity outside the bloodline, the *Ramayana* and the *Mahabharata* both offer us unforgettable examples of sacrificial fraternity within a clan. No one who has heard the Ram–Lakshman and the Ram–Bharat stories can fully shake off their impact. The same is true of the *Mahabharata*'s narration of how, at his death, Yudhishthir chooses hell with his brothers over heaven without them.

Recorded history too offers powerful lessons. Long ago, in the third century BCE, Ashoka spelt out an essential aspect of fraternity. The emperor's 12th Major Rock Edict proclaims:

> One should honour another man's sect, for by so doing one increases the influence of one's own sect and benefits that of the other man... Whosoever honours his own sect or disparages that of another man harms his own sect even more seriously... Concord is to be commended, so that men may hear one another's principles.

If 'sect' in these words is also taken to include 'caste' or 'race', what we have in Ashoka's 12th Major Rock Edict are common-sense prescriptions, valid even for our times, for solidarity within a nation and also for friendship across frontiers: 'Listen to one another.' 'Honour one another.'

We bow before you, Ashoka!

~

Yet crucial questions must be asked. If over time Indians were touched by pictures of fraternity in some locations, or heartened by hints elsewhere of democratic exercises, whether in a *sabha* here or a *parishad* there, does it follow that India's polity was essentially democratic for impressive lengths of time? The answer can only be that any such conclusion would require plenty of additional evidence.

It should also be asked, was India's society generally marked by respect for everyone's dignity? If not continuously, at least for substantial periods?

Sadly, enquiries like these do not fetch confident answers in the positive. Whether the question is about polity or the people, India's past does not reveal democracy with consistency or on a meaningful scale.

When, as one century followed another, we look at actual Indian society around the pillars and rocks that contain Ashoka's edicts, or at real life in the villages and cities where Ram's brotherly feelings towards Guha the low-caste boatman are cited, we are likely to find neglect, indifference and contempt towards the low castes, the outcastes and the Adivasis.

There's also this nagging question: how often, when we stare at our past, do we find a long-lasting Indian state, kingdom or empire? If for extended periods there was no substantial Indian state or kingdom, where was the question of a democratic polity? That illustrious historian, R.C. Majumdar, is no doubt right when he says that those bemoaning the scarcity of enduring periods of statehood in India's long history often disregard our country's extreme physical, religious, racial and linguistic variety.

As Majumdar puts it, 'India cannot be looked upon as a country in the same sense in which we apply the term to modern European countries like France or Germany... It will be unreasonable to look for that unity in Indian history which the annals of a country like France or Italy afford. Such unity may be expected only in kingdoms like Magadha, Gauda, Kosala, Surasena, Avanti and Karnata...'[12]

Sadly, however, the remarkable unity that these more homogeneous (and usually smaller) regions found in our past did not last for long. And while a very old inscription in one corner of the country may lay down stunning democratic rules for conducting a village-level meeting, and an ancient text elsewhere may prescribe modern-sounding procedures for discussion in a conference of Buddhist monks, the limited evidence that is available of this kind cannot establish the prevalence of democracy over a significant and continuous period of time in any region.

To a few in India, ideas of democracy, and of republicanism, were indeed known more than a couple of millennia ago. However, the vast majority of the population, including those who grew grain, or raised cattle, or wove cloth, or pushed loads on India's rough paths, or removed carcasses, or toiled in other ways across the broad territory of India—*they* did not taste democracy. They surely tasted precious bonds with some others, but almost always those were bonds within a family, *jati*, or tribe, and seemed often joined to an aversion to, or from, fellow humans beyond their small circle.

There was separation, there was gradation, there was contempt, there was aversion. Clinging, down the centuries, to caste, Indian society had legitimized, in Ambedkar's unforgettable phrase, an 'ascending scale of reverence and a descending scale of contempt'.[13]

And there was untouchability! Before the Buddha, and after him. It's there still, in 2024, whatever the Constitution and its abolition-of-untouchability article might say.

~

To go back to ancient or legendary times, there is also the Krishna–Sudama story. Perhaps there are some who are not stirred by it. I must confess that it moves me each time I return to it. Yet there's a word in that story that makes me pause and wonder.

We are told that Sudama, Krishna's boyhood friend in an ashram school, is poor and diffident. We're told further that Sudama is a poor Brahmin. When I stop there, it's not because a Brahmin cannot be poor or apprehensive. Of course she or he can. I stop there because even this immortal story of Krishna and Sudama brings up caste.

We know that Sudama is defined by his poverty, by his early friendship with Krishna, by his diffidence, by the unexpected miracle that in the end blesses him and his wife—*and by his caste*. In this case, by the highest caste.

The Sudama story inspires. It elicits tears. It adds to faith. But if you are not a Brahmin, and the preponderant majority of Indians are not, it can also wound. The Sudama story explains why India's psychological and spiritual climate, reflected in our history and culture and also formed by our history and culture (we may also call it, in fewer words, our *social climate*) is both wonderfully conducive to fraternity and hurtfully destructive of it.

Porbandar, where Gandhi was born, is also known as Sudamapuri, for legend links Sudama to that port city on our western coast. And Gandhi, we know, is linked to two haunting words from a beautiful song. That song, of course, is '*Vaishnava Jana*', and the two words that linger long after they've been sung are *peed paraayi*—the pain of the outsider, which is something the Sudama story does *not* capture.

Peed paraayi are the words that leap up before us the moment *Vaishnava Jana*'s opening note, played on any instrument, reaches our ears. If caste is part of India's air, the notion that we should feel the stranger's pain has also powerfully entered that air—thanks to Mohandas Gandhi, born in the nineteenth century, thanks to blessed Narsi Mehta, born in the fifteenth, who wrote *Vaishnava Jana* on that stretch of our western coast, and no doubt thanks also to several predecessors, contemporaries and successors of these two.

Thanks, in other words, to poets or other individuals who paused, looked around, saw neglect, oppression and pain, wept, reflected, and shared with the rest of us what their hearts had told them.

Having embraced *Vaishnava Jana* in his boyhood, Gandhi in later years was always perfectly happy, we know, to have the song modified if anyone pointed out that knowing the outsider's pain was the mark not merely of the true Vaishnava but also of the true Shaiva, the true Muslim, the true Christian, the true Sikh, the true Parsi, the true Buddhist, the true Jew...

On that famous eighth day of August 1942, when Gandhi summoned fellow Indians to join him in asking the British to quit their rule over India, he not only began with the *Vaishnava Jana* song, he took care to recall his close British friend who had died two years earlier, Charlie Andrews, as also the British viceroy at that time, Lord Linlithgow, and Linlithgow's daughter and son-in-law, whom Gandhi had sought to befriend.[14] Even when he firmly challenged them, 'outsiders' remained part of Gandhi's family of concern. To him, this recognition was part of fraternity.

~

Although some would rather look away, we're all aware that among the more than 1.4 billion who inhabit today's India, three large communities lead particularly troubled lives: one, the bottom-rung castes; two, the Adivasis; and three, the religious minorities.

In a famous recent book, the American author, Isabel Wilkerson, imagining a building where all of America lives, focused on the crowded basement into which that country's African Americans are packed. We can acknowledge that

Indian society, similarly, has its own dingy basement, which is crammed with the great bulk of our religious minorities, our low castes and outcastes, and our Adivasis.

Throughout history, India has been a land of multiple races. If today around forty million people of Indian origin reside outside India, earlier periods saw people moving *into* India from other places. The previously quoted eminent historian, R.C. Majumdar, cites and agrees with what he calls 'the authoritative view' of another scholar, B.S. Guha, that 'no less than six racial elements have contributed to build up the population of India'.[15]

You don't need to be a specialist in physiognomy to notice the rich variety in India of faces and races. Our eyes bump into this variety every day. Moreover, the simplest ear is struck by the diversity in the languages we speak. And it's impossible to miss the wide range of our religions. What Abul Kalam Azad said eloquently in 1940 has been felt by others who have reflected on the question:

> It was India's historic destiny that many human races and cultures and religions should flow to her, finding a home in her hospitable soil, and that many a caravan should find rest here. Even before the dawn of history, these caravans trekked into India, and wave after wave of newcomers followed. This vast and fertile land gave welcome to all, and took them to her bosom.[16]

If variety among its people has been India's *age-old* characteristic, *European rule* stamped new features during the eighteenth, nineteenth and twentieth centuries, reshaping the country's psychological and social climate.

In broad terms, it may be asserted that British rule (whether or not 'British' equals 'European' makes little difference to most Indians) added both to Indian unity *and* to India's divisions. As the British consolidated their rule, Indians were brought closer to one another in a single subcontinental state where procedures and the law became uniform across the land. Other innovations also emerged that enhanced unity among Indians. These included the railways, the telegraph, the universities, all-India military and civil services that translocated Indians across vast distances, and the creation of an all-India community, unquestionably elitist, of English-knowing Indians.

This is as much a historical fact as the humiliation that imperialism caused, and the theft that imperialism enabled. Just as importantly, or even more importantly, Indians brought closer to one another by the innovations of alien rule *were glad to come together in order to oppose alien rule.* Resentment of alien rule became a cementing force that Robert Clive, whose triumphs in eighteenth-century battles helped establish British rule over India, or his immediate successors may not have anticipated.

To complete this summarized and mixed picture, let

us record imperialism's blatant recourse to divide-and-rule. Two quotations from a large bundle should suffice.

In 1861, four years after the Great Revolt of 1857, Charles Wood, secretary of state for India in London, wrote to Canning, the viceroy in India, about the necessity of divide-and-rule among the soldiers who were being recruited and trained: 'If one regiment mutinies, the next regiment [should be] so alien that it would be ready to fire into it.'[17]

In 1939, after the Second World War began, and the Indian National Congress asked the British for a commitment on post-war independence for India before it could promise cooperation, Viceroy Linlithgow, to quote from his letter to King George VI, 'invited representatives of all the more important interests and communities in India' not aligned with the INC, 'including the Chancellor of the Chamber of Princes and Mr Jinnah' for personal conversations. 'It was a heavy and trying task,' the Viceroy added, 'but well worth the trouble.'[18]

Long after Britain's departure from India, divide-and-rule continues to exact its price. However, we should also recall the truth in Muhammad Ali Jauhar's 1930 remark in London. Addressing the British, that peppery Oxford-educated freedom-fighter from UP's Rampur had said: 'The Hindu–Muslim problem is of your creation. But not altogether. It is the old maxim of divide-and-rule. But there is a division of labour. *We* divide and *you* rule.'[19]

What the foregoing lines suggest is that fraternity or solidarity is not a quality that naturally, inevitably or continually governs relationships among India's diverse groups. It does not seem to be a tree that grows by itself, or a stream that flows by itself. It seems to require assistance from humans—from India's inhabitants and rulers.

~

In the following chapter we will look in greater detail at the history that eventually resulted in the insertion of fraternity in our Preamble. In many ways, this history is also the history of remarkable efforts that were made in the first half of the twentieth century to create solidarity in India's society as well as political alliances for India's freedom.

We can start a preliminary discussion here by acknowledging a couple of obvious truths. Given the priceless dignity of a single human life, none of the three broad groups who inhabit India's basement can be seen as being more or less important than the other two, or more or less important than those living above the basement. Moreover, each 'group' on any floor contains scores of inner groups. We should retain this understanding.

Everyone knows of the centrality to India's life of the Hindu–Muslim relationship. This 'H–M' story, as some like to call it, doesn't just influence society and politics within India. The H–M relationship is crucial to India's life and commerce in the vast geographical region to which India belongs. Muslims are either predominant, dominant or influential (close to or more than a fifth of the population) in the following zones: (1) South Asia; (2) the Gulf; (3) the Middle East (West Asia); (4) Central Asia; (5) Southeast Asia; (6) West Africa; (7) North Africa; and (8) East Africa. (Muslims make up around 45 per cent of the population of all of Africa.)

Islam came to India both by sea and by land, starting with our land's southern, western and northern portions. Traders from the Arab world carried Islam to our shores. Invaders from Central Asia brought Islam to the plains.

The bulk of 'foreign' Muslims came to India about one *thousand* years ago or earlier. If, despite more than a millennium of shared habitation, Islam and Christianity (which probably entered India even before Islam did) are to be seen as 'foreign' or 'alien' religions in India, then Buddhism has to be a 'foreign' or 'alien' religion in Japan, China, Sri Lanka, Myanmar, Thailand, Vietnam and elsewhere, and Hinduism a 'foreign' or 'alien' religion in the US, the UK, Canada, Australia, and elsewhere. We can also ask whether Hinduism in Nepal is a native or a foreign religion.

When 'foreigners' make another country their home, they, and certainly their descendants, become native. In our times, Rishi Sunak is a Brit, not a foreigner in the UK.

Kamala Harris is an American, not an alien in the US. Centuries ago, Akbar and Shah Jahan were Indians, not foreigners.

Nonetheless, not long after the first 'foreign' Muslims made India their home, and a community of Muslims joined our land's other communities, a divide began that should be recognized and frontally faced. Giving pride of place to *belief*, a sharp distinction was drawn from the Muslim side between Muslims praying before an unborn and eternal Almighty God who had created the earth and its inhabitants, and Hindus praying before idols imagined as divinities.

Recognition by a few influential Muslims that Hindus too were petitioning none other than Almighty God, and merely seeking an idol's aid to do so, did not alter a popular Muslim perception of Hindu idolatry.

Giving pride of place to *birth*, devout Hindus, on the other hand, drew a sharp distinction between those like themselves who were born on India's sacred soil or into a privileged caste, and others, like the Muslims, who were not so fortunate. 'Belief' and 'Birth' confronted each other. 'Their belief is inferior,' thought the Muslim. 'Their birth is inferior,' thought the Hindu. Sometimes such thoughts were expressed in speech or writing.

Most of the time, however, there was tolerance and understanding between Hindus and Muslims. On the street, Hindus and Muslims often joined in celebrating one another's religious festivals, or sold things to one another. Sometimes Hindus and Muslims worked in the same *karkhana*, or sat in the same boat or cart. Or, in more recent times, inside the same train, and, some decades later, in the same cinema hall.

However, entry into the homes of neighbours linked to the other faith was rare and remained rare, and breaking bread together was rarer still.

Peace on the street did not prevent a Muslim from looking down at the faith of his Hindu neighbour as polytheistic or idolatrous, or a Hindu from cleaning with extra energy a cup from which a Muslim visitor might have drunk water. These were attitudes or customs that prevented a deeper unity. Even among people of goodwill, sentiments were frequently wounded.

From century to century, on the other hand, teachers, thinkers, poets or singers surfaced in virtually every part of our land—from every caste of India's mass of humanity and from both the H–M worlds—to underline the essential similarity in all human beings, no matter their beliefs, no matter where they were born. The individuals, who pointed this out over the last twelve or so centuries, using one language after another from a large cultural store, include, among a host of others, Guru Nanak, Baba Farid, Bulleh Shah, and Waris Shah from Punjab; Kashmir's Lal Ded;

Ajmer's Muinuddin Chishti; Delhi's Qutbuddin Kaki and Nizamuddin Auliya; Rajasthan's Mira; western UP's Surdas; Gujarat's Narsi Mehta and Dadu; Maharashtra's Dnyaneswar, Namdev, Eknath, Tukaram and Ramdas; the Kashi-nourished Ramanand, Kabir, Tulsidas and Ravidas; the south's Sankara, Ramanuja, Valluvar, Basava, Purandaradasa, Andal, Akka Mahadevi and Avvaiyar; Bengal's Chaitanya; and Assam's Sankar Dev.

Many of these poet-saints thought of their fellow inhabitants the way that Ram thought, in the *Ramayana*, of Guha the low-caste boatman or of Ravan's brother Vibhishan. 'They are *my brothers*.' Or *my sisters*. Tended by gardeners like the ones we've recalled, fraternity strengthened its roots in India and grew.

India, true, has seldom been fully democratic. For centuries it prevented the application of fraternity to caste or gender. Nonetheless, thanks to the Buddha, Nanak, the Bhakti and Sufi saints and others walking their paths, it elevated the idea of fraternity between ordinary people practising their different religious faiths.

~

In more recent times, from the 1940s onwards, Indian cinema did for Hindu–Muslim friendship what the poet-saints had done in earlier centuries. Hardly a film appeared that did not have both Hindu and Muslim stars. Some stars, female and male, bore Hindu names even though everyone knew they were Muslim. Almost always the storyline revealed the stupidity of prejudice and the joys of acceptance.

And the songs! Rendered by Hindu and Muslim singers, often possessing an ageless appeal, their lyrics penned by brilliant poets, again both Muslim and Hindu, those songs disseminated lines and notes that would be hummed by Indians to the end of their lives, no matter who they were or where in the world they were living or dying. The songs' lines were about romance, longing, separation—human emotions felt alike by Hindus and Muslims and by those who were neither.

At least some students of Indian history may concede that from the 1940s to the 1980s Indian cinema brought as much good health to India's psychological, spiritual and social climate as the great Bhakti and Sufi poets had done in earlier centuries. Films enlivened and deepened the sense that Indians belonged to one another.

~

Mahatma Gandhi was not a watcher of films. In his entire life he may not have seen more than a handful. But he too did what cinema had done—he strengthened fraternity.

More than one hundred years ago, in 1919, a year that saw great levels of H–M partnership—the year also of the Jallianwala Bagh massacre where the blood of Hindus,

Muslims and Sikhs merged as it soaked the Amritsar ground—Gandhi asked Hindus and Muslims to 'declare with God as their witness that we shall behave towards one another as children of the same parents, that the sorrows of each shall be the sorrows of the other and that each shall help the other in removing them'.[20]

Again and again, for thirty-three continuous years, Indians heard from Gandhi that Hindus and Muslims were neighbours, brothers, members of the same human family, and of the same Indian family. When, in 1939–40, Partition was demanded, Gandhi replied that 'it was worse than anarchy to partition a poor country...whose every corner is populated by Hindus and Muslims living side by side'.

'A Bengali Muslim', said Gandhi, 'speaks the same tongue that a Bengali Hindu does, eats the same food, has the same amusements as his Hindu neighbour. They dress alike.' 'How are the Muslims of the Punjab different', Gandhi continued, 'from the Hindus and the Sikhs? Are they not all Punjabis, drinking the same water, breathing the same air and deriving sustenance from the same soil?'[21]

When, despite Gandhi's dissent, Partition was accepted by Nehru, Patel and virtually all of his lifelong colleagues, Gandhi continued to ask for fraternity among the people and across the new borders. In the poisoned climate of that 1947 summer, someone once asked him whether a mad dog should not be killed. Replying that he knew that what the questioner really wanted to know was 'what should be done when *a man* went mad', Gandhi related an incident from his boyhood:

> I remember when I was about ten, a brother of mine had gone mad. Afterwards he was cured. He is no more... In a fit of madness, he would rush out and strike everyone. But what could I do to him? Could I beat him? Or could my mother or father beat him? ... A vaidya was called in and he was asked to treat my brother in every possible manner except by beating him. He was my blood-brother. But now I make no such distinctions. Now all of you are like my blood-brothers. If all of you lose your sanity and I happen to have an army at my disposal, do you think I should have you shot?[22]

That was the key thought: *All of you are like my blood brothers.*

In the afternoon of 18 January 1948, twelve days before he would be assassinated, representatives of Delhi's citizens promised Gandhi that they would keep the capital peaceful. Thereupon Gandhi, who had been fasting for six days to restore amity, agreed to sip from a glass of orange juice that Abul Kalam Azad handed to him. An hour or so later, he composed a statement:

> 'They have assured me,' said Gandhi, 'that from now on Hindus, Sikhs and Muslims will live as brothers and under no conditions and on no provocation will

> the residents of Delhi, including the refugees, become enemies of each other. This is not a small thing...
>
> '[W]e must pledge', he added, 'that once we have turned our face towards God we shall never turn away. When that happens India and Pakistan will unitedly be able to serve the world and make the world nobler. I do not wish to live for any other purpose.'[23]

Looking back, we can see that in 1947–48, as India and Pakistan found freedom but also confronted the poison of ill-will, Gandhi's indefatigable voice of goodwill reached leaders as well as millions of ordinary men and women, bolstering life and dignity.

Moreover, a crucial part was played by unknown citizens—by quiet, compassionate and ingenious neighbours. Although many innocent lives were harshly put to an end during that wild season, those who somehow protected the vulnerable Other greatly exceeded, in both India and Pakistan, the count of killers. That was the largely untold story of the 1947 summer and autumn.

We all know, however, that in more recent years, starting in the mid-1980s and accelerating from 2014, the pull of Hindu supremacy has strongly influenced India's social climate, damaging equality, dignity and democracy, and unhappily Pakistan seems to face as hard or even harder challenges.

~

Begun in 1885 with the formation of the Indian National Congress, India's political movement for independence had commenced with a demand for the inclusion of Indians in local or provincial councils. At first only involving professional elites in leading cities, the INC steadily broadened its base, acquired a mass character in 1920, and became a major factor in India's political and social climate.

Its doors opening to people of different backgrounds, the INC chose Hindu, Muslim and Christian presidents from its early years. In 1917, a woman of Irish descent, Annie Besant, was elected to the chair, and in 1925 another woman became president—the poet Sarojini Naidu, who had Bengali and Telugu connections. And although it was only in 1960, well after Independence, that the INC chose its first Dalit president (Andhra's D. Sanjivayya), the body had declared in 1920 that the abolition of untouchability was its goal.

While the INC's sustained efforts took the ideas of freedom and democracy to the country's remotest corners, two observations seem fair. One, compared with the goals of equality and fraternity in Indian society, independence from British rule elicited greater enthusiasm from the Indian people. Two, the INC itself was highly energetic when it was creating fervour in the Indian population for ending British rule, and much less so when it came to building fraternity and equality in Indian society.

In 1921, Tagore seems to have spoken as follows to Gandhi: 'You have persuaded Muslim and Hindu to sit side by side on the political platform and to crack a whip together at the British Raj... But how far down in their hearts and minds does this sense of unity...penetrate?'[24]

More than a century later, in 2024, the question continues to remain relevant. And identical questions can be asked about ground-level intermingling involving caste or tribal groups. How widespread or deep is this intermingling? How actively are individuals and organizations fostering it? Are we, the people of India, progressing towards partnership and a shared life? Is eventual equality and fusion our aim?

Those are tough questions, but perhaps necessary ones. While pondering them, we should return to our enquiry into modern history. In the chapter that follows, we will look at the journey which, in retrospect, led to our Constitution and its Preamble, and to the insertion in the latter of 'fraternity'.

Chapter IV

Fraternity and the Indian Constitution

The previous chapter noted that as its annual presidents the Indian National Congress, launched in Mumbai in 1885, wisely chose Muslim, Christian and Parsi individuals as well as Hindus. While this showed awareness of the need for national solidarity, we should recall a remark that Pune's Jotiba Phule made shortly after the INC's opening session.

Born into a lowly peasant caste and focusing, along with his wife Savitri, on educating children, especially girls, from the humblest families, Phule (1827–1890) had arrived at a simple conclusion: all human beings were members of a single family. Following the INC's launch, Phule said that the Congress could become national only if it addressed the hardships of the peasants and the Dalits and if it was 'formed of men of all religions'.[25]

About twenty-five years after Phule's comment, the

INC, influenced by Gandhi's successful struggles on behalf of farmers in Bihar and Gujarat, embraced the peasantry. In 1920, as mentioned previously, the INC also resolved to make the abolition of untouchability a central goal. As for the pivotal 'religious' question, Gandhi had squarely confronted it eleven years earlier, in his 1909 text *Hind Swaraj*:

> 'India cannot cease to be one nation', wrote Gandhi, 'because people belonging to different religions live in it... Those who are conscious of the spirit of nationality do not interfere with one another's religion.
>
> 'If the Hindus believe that India should be peopled only by Hindus, they are living in dreamland. The Hindus, the Muslims, the Parsis and the Christians who have made India their country are fellow countrymen, and they will have to live in unity, if only for their own interest.
>
> 'Is the God of the Muslim different from the God of the Hindu? ... There are deadly proverbs as between the followers of Siva and those of Vishnu, yet nobody suggests that these two do not belong to the same nation. It is said that the Vedic religion is different from Jainism, but the followers of the respective faiths are not different nations.
>
> 'In no part of the world are one nationality and one religion synonymous terms; nor has it ever been so in India...'[26]

This was an unequivocal commitment to equality and fraternity. It also revealed a grasp that human rights or fundamental rights were not merely a matter between the people and their government, whether native or alien. Rights were also a matter among and between the people.

~

In 1927, challenged by the Empire to produce a constitution which much of a seemingly sharply divided Indian public would be willing to endorse, the Indian National Congress set up a panel chaired by Motilal Nehru to draw up precisely such a document. Apart from the brilliant lawyer, Tej Bahadur Sapru, this panel also included two gifted and popular young leaders, Jawaharlal Nehru, who was 38 at the time, and 30-year-old Subhas Bose, as also two prominent Muslim figures, Ali Imam and Shuaib Qureshi.

In due course, the fundamental rights proposed by this Motilal Nehru committee would enter the core of India's constitution. In the late 1920s, however, the Muslim League, headed by the Karachi-born Gujarati, Muhammad Ali Jinnah (1876–1948), rejected as insufficient the Nehru panel's proposal on the 'religious' question, which was to reserve, for the Muslims of undivided India, a quarter of the central assembly's seats, and a related proposal to reserve seats in provincial legislatures for any religious minority constituting ten per cent or more of the population.

An independent Supreme Court, linguistic provinces, and Hindustani (written in Devanagari or Urdu) as the official language were some of the Nehru panel's other recommendations. Viewed now, after almost a century, the ideas, taken as a whole, suggest a serious effort for a workable compromise.

An important element in the Muslim League's rejection of the Nehru proposals was the question of provincial autonomy. The League did not want a strong, Hindu-dominated centre to possess undue influence over two huge Muslim-majority provinces: Bengal and Punjab. The future would show that this 'federal' question, i.e. the relationship between state governments and the centre, would not be restricted to the insecurities of religious minorities. A range of issues—including the allocation of tax revenues, authority over bureaucrats, the right to river waters, the demarcation of state boundaries, and the language of communication between governments—would test the relationship between a state and the central government or between neighbouring states.

Another milestone in India's constitutional history was a resolution on fundamental rights which the INC adopted in Karachi in 1931. Held after the nationwide resistance, triggered by the Salt March, of the year 1930, during which, in Winston Churchill's words, Indians had 'inflicted such humiliation and defiance as has not been known since the

British first trod the soil of India',[27] this Karachi session was presided over by Vallabhbhai Patel.

Leaders present in Karachi from across India included Khan Abdul Ghaffar Khan, whose unarmed Khudai Khidmatgars had in the previous year immobilized the Empire's guns in the Frontier Province, and the radical Subhas Bose, who was impatient for complete independence from British rule. Also present were the spirits of Bhagat Singh, Rajguru and Sukhdev, who on the session's eve had been hanged by the Empire for the killing of a British police officer.

Collaboration between Jawaharlal Nehru and Gandhi produced the text of Karachi's resolution on fundamental rights,[28] which Gandhi moved on 31 March 1931. A key marker towards a future constitution, this resolution committed the Congress to ensuring, after independence, the freedoms of expression, religion, thought and assembly; the abolition of untouchability and serfdom; equality, regardless of caste, sex or creed; a minimum wage and limited working hours; and a secular state. 'Swaraj will favour Hinduism no more than Islam, nor Islam more than Hinduism,' Gandhi explained.[29]

~

What followed in the next eighteen months was the epic Gandhi–Ambedkar face-off, ending in what history knows as the 'Poona Pact' of September 1932.

This confrontation, reflecting a tension between national independence and social justice but also enabling the two men to get to know each other better, was played out in two venues. The first location was a Round Table Conference held in London in the 1931 autumn. (An earlier RTC had taken place in 1930.) At the RTC, the British prime minister and his colleagues discussed the possibility of Indian independence with leaders from India.

The second site was a prison in Pune where, following the RTC's failure and resumption of resistance by him and the INC, Gandhi had been confined by the Empire, and where Ambedkar went to meet him in September 1932.

It was a classic debate between two men fighting for the dignity and freedom of their people. The younger man wanted the liberation of India's Dalits from chains imposed for centuries by a harsh society. The older man wanted the unity of all Indians to achieve their liberation from nearly two centuries of uninvited and often oppressive alien rule. Each wanted the world to know what was at stake. In one case, it was India's slavery or freedom; in the other, the right of India's untouchables to be seen as human beings.

In 1927, as a rising leader of the untouchables, Ambedkar had mobilized over 10,000 of his people in Mahad, about 170 kilometres south of Mumbai, for a satyagraha for access to water from a public tank. By calling his resistance a satyagraha, Ambedkar was acknowledging precedents from

Gandhi, whose portrait was displayed in Mahad. Ambedkar and the others marched to the tank and drank forbidden water. Greatly offended, Mahad's Brahmins arranged a ritual to restore the tank's purity.

However, Ambedkar's warmth towards Gandhi would dwindle. The latter's unwillingness to frontally oppose the caste system annoyed Ambedkar, who also felt that leadership in the anti-untouchability struggle should belong to the untouchables. Gandhi, who needed caste Hindus for the freedom struggle, could not afford to alienate them completely. He also thought that as important as Dalit struggle was caste Hindu repentance and caste Hindu involvement in Dalit progress.

The two had much in common, however, including an awareness that independence could strengthen caste Hindu domination. Not long before leaving for the London RTC, Gandhi had offered this sobering prognosis in Ahmedabad:

> If we came into power with the stain of untouchability unaffected, I am positive that the [situation of the] 'untouchables' would be far worse under that 'swaraj' than they are now, for the simple reason that our weaknesses and our failings would then be buttressed by the accession of power.[30]

Ambedkar had held this view for some time. Nevertheless, the RTC saw a bitter clash between Gandhi and Ambedkar. Demanding a separate electorate and reserved seats for the untouchables, Ambedkar challenged Gandhi's right to speak for his people, even as Muslim delegates to the RTC, disowning Gandhi's leadership, insisted on a separate Muslim electorate.

Gandhi was in no position to reject a separate Muslim electorate, which had been formally accepted in the Congress–League Pact signed in Lucknow in 1916 by Tilak and Annie Besant for the Congress, and by Jinnah and others for the Muslim League.

But a separate electorate for Dalits was contrary to all that Gandhi had hitherto worked for. In his own life, and for a widening circle, Gandhi had smashed the barrier of untouchability. Along with other reformist Hindus, he had also built a slender bridge on which caste Hindus and untouchables were courageously walking. A separate electorate would restore the barrier, weaken the bridge, and reverse the reform process.

Worst of all, thought Gandhi, a separate electorate would 'divide the Hindu community into armed camps' and expose Dalits to greater hostility. In a London discussion held outside the RTC (in Friends House, the Quaker centre), Gandhi spoke frankly:

> The untouchables are in the hands of superior classes. They can suppress them completely and wreak vengeance upon the untouchables who are at their mercy. I may be opening out my shame to you. But...how can I invite

> utter destruction for them? I would not be guilty of that crime.[31]

But how far would caste Hindu reform actually go? Looking at the India around him, Ambedkar saw few signs of actual change. He wasn't going to rely on imagined reforms. For Dalits, he wanted a share in governance based on law, independent of caste Hindu goodwill or magnanimity.

Others invited to the RTC, including leaders of Muslim parties and prominent rulers of princely states, also spoke of the dangers of majority dominance. In the end, several RTC delegates, including Ambedkar and the Aga Khan, entered into a Minorities' Pact and successfully prevented an endorsement of the INC's demand, articulated by Gandhi, for immediate dominion status for India.

The Minorities' Pact demanded separate electorates in Indian legislatures for Muslims, Dalits, Christians, Anglo-Indians and India-based Europeans. Arguing that a separate electorate for Dalits means 'the perpetual bar sinister', Gandhi told the RTC on 13 November:

> I would not sell the vital interests of the untouchables even for the sake of winning the freedom of India... Today there is a body of Hindu reformers who are pledged to remove the blot of untouchability. Sikhs may remain as such in perpetuity, so may Mohammedans, so may Europeans. Will untouchables remain untouchables in perpetuity?

Speaking of 'the two divisions' in every village that separate electorates would entrench, Gandhi suggested that those demanding separation 'do not know their India, do not know how Indian society is today constructed'. He ended with a declaration: 'I want to say with all the emphasis that I can command that if I was the only person to resist this thing, I would resist it with my life.'[32]

~

When the RTC ended in failure, Gandhi and the INC resumed their struggle for independence, and thousands including Gandhi were again imprisoned. On 17 August 1932, by when he had spent over eight months in Pune's Yerawada Jail, Gandhi learnt of London's decision—HMG's Award, as it was called—that in future voting in India, the Dalits, then termed the Depressed Classes by the government, would form a separate electorate.

The next day, Gandhi cabled Prime Minister Ramsay MacDonald that he was going to 'resist your decision with my life'. Unless the decision was revised, explained Gandhi, he would cease taking food from midday on 20 September.

Gandhi was challenging MacDonald and Ambedkar—and India's caste Hindus. In Yerawada, Gandhi told fellow prisoners Vallabhbhai Patel and Mahadev Desai that he wished to 'sting the Hindu conscience'.[33] If caste Hindus were unwilling to end their disdain of Dalits, they should be willing, said Gandhi, to let him die. On the other hand, if they were prepared to alter their attitudes, Ambedkar might give up his insistence on separate electorates, thereby compelling MacDonald's cabinet to withdraw its decision.

Wanting Ambedkar to drop a strongly held stand, Gandhi, on his part, was willing to forgo something himself. To secure Ambedkar's assent to a common electorate, Gandhi was prepared to change an earlier stand and accept reserved seats for Dalits in India's legislatures.

Moreover, Gandhi was clear that in numbers the seats reserved for Dalits should accord with their ratio in the population. Which worked out to about twice the seats contemplated in HMG's Award. However, Gandhi wanted Dalit legislators to be elected by a general electorate, not by Dalits alone, and to represent everyone in their constituencies.

Caste Hindus were shaken on 12 September 1932, when Gandhi's correspondence with MacDonald was released to the press. Telegrams piled up at Yerawada, Downing Street and the Viceroy's House in New Delhi. The orthodox Brahmin leader, Madan Mohan Malaviya, based in Varanasi, summoned Hindu leaders to a conference in Mumbai. Mass meetings across India urged Gandhi to withdraw his fast and MacDonald to change his award.

A telegraphed plea against the fast came from C. Rajagopalachari, who, Patel being in prison, was acting as the Congress president. Replied Gandhi: 'I expect you to rejoice that a comrade has a God-given opportunity for a final act of satyagraha in the cause of the downtrodden'.[34]

In other messages to caste Hindus, Gandhi claimed that this was but the beginning. Henceforth, he claimed, 'an increasing army' of reformers would resist 'social, civic and political persecution of the Depressed Classes'. Asserting that the issue was of 'transcendental value, far surpassing Swaraj', Gandhi said he wanted his cry to reach 'the throne of Almighty God'.[35]

Once the fast started, the Empire permitted negotiators and relatives to visit Gandhi—the fast had opened prison locks. Gandhi's wife Kasturba was allowed to leave her prison and join her fasting husband in his. Recovering from typhoid in another prison, Gandhi's youngest son Devadas was released too. He declared that he would rather 'forfeit his father's life' than see the suppressed classes injured.

Rabindranath Tagore arrived from eastern India to see the fasting Gandhi, who lay on a jail bed under a mango tree in the Yerawada compound, and for some minutes buried 'his face in the clothes on Gandhiji's breast'. Malaviya and Rajagopalachari also showed up.

So did Ambedkar (and other leaders of the Depressed Classes, including M.C. Rajah and P.N. Rajbhoj). Ambedkar's first words were, 'Mahatmaji, you have been very unfair to us.' 'It is always my lot to appear to be unfair,' Gandhi replied. According to Gandhi's close associate and future biographer, Pyarelal, who had also arrived in Yerawada, 'The redoubtable Doctor [Ambedkar], strongly supported by his colleagues, fought every inch of the ground.'[36]

The fast undoubtedly put pressure on Ambedkar, who understood well the implications of letting Gandhi die. Yet Ambedkar's firmness had secured Gandhi's reversal on reservation. Gandhi's clarity that the Dalits should get their full share of seats had further reduced the gap between the two.

Orthodoxy felt greater pressure. Yielding to it, temples closed for ages to Dalits opened their doors. In city after city, Brahmins and Dalits dined together. Tagore thought that a 'wonder' was 'happening before our very eyes'.[37]

On the evening of 24 September, Dalit and caste Hindu leaders signed the Poona Pact. Malaviya signed first, followed by Ambedkar, who was followed by Rajagopalachari and Rajendra Prasad. Dalit leaders Rajah, Srinivasan and Gavai also signed.

Since Gandhi's condition had entered the danger zone, word of the agreement was cabled to London, where MacDonald and his ministers implemented it, modifying their earlier award. At 5 pm on the 26th, after news of the alteration had reached Yerawada, Gandhi broke his fast, sipping orange juice handed to him by a relieved Kasturba, with Tagore present.

By this time, meeting in Mumbai in response to Malaviya's initiative, out-of-prison Hindu leaders had made a historic pledge. On 25 September, they resolved that 'one of the earliest Acts of the Swaraj Parliament' would be to assure to Dalits equal access to 'public wells, public schools, public roads and all other public institutions'.[38] It was a commitment that Ambedkar recorded.[39]

Gandhi's acceptance of reserved seats was matched, in the Poona Pact, by the acceptance of a common electorate by Ambedkar and other Dalit leaders. Incorporated later in free India's elections and legislatures, the agreement has endured, surviving the charge that fear of caste Hindu reprisals on Dalits had forced Ambedkar to accept what he was against.

That suggestion is belied by records of the 1932 fast and the negotiations that followed. Ambedkar said at the time that he had been 'surprised, immensely surprised' to find 'so much in common' between Gandhi and himself. 'If you devoted yourself entirely to the welfare of the Depressed Classes,' Ambedkar added, 'you would become our hero'.[40]

For all his later criticism of Gandhi, Ambedkar never charged, in 1932 or thereafter, that the terms of the Poona Pact were coerced out of him against his better judgement. He knew, moreover, that conservative Hindus saw Gandhi's fast as pressure on them and resented the Pact that followed. While observing that 'the Untouchables were sad' because of the concessions that he had made, Ambedkar would add that 'the caste Hindus very definitely disliked [the Pact], although they had not the courage to reject it'.[41]

These remarks were made in 1945 in Ambedkar's book, *What Congress and Gandhi Have Done to the Untouchables* (Bombay: Thacker, 1945), where he criticized Gandhi's 1932 fast and the working out of the Poona Pact, but not the terms of that pact. Claiming the Pact as a victory, Ambedkar wrote in this book that Gandhi was 'obliged to sign a pact—called the Poona Pact—which conceded the political demands of the Untouchables...'[42]

On his part, Gandhi said that he saw 'the hand of God' in 'the glorious manifestation throughout the length and breadth of India during the past seven days'. Expressing his gratitude to Ambedkar and the other Dalit leaders endorsing the pact, Gandhi added:

> They could have taken up an uncompromising and defiant attitude by way of punishment to the so-called caste Hindus for the sins of generations.
>
> If they had done so, I at least could not have resented their attitude and my death would have been but a trifling price exacted for the tortures that the outcastes of Hinduism have been going through for unknown generations. But they chose a nobler path and have thus shown that they have followed the precept of forgiveness enjoined by all religions. Let me hope that

> the caste Hindus will prove themselves worthy of this forgiveness...[43]

To fellow caste Hindus, Gandhi addressed blunt remarks:

> The political part of [the settlement]...occupies but a small space in the vast field of reform that has to be tackled by caste Hindus during the coming days, namely, the complete removal of social and religious disabilities under which a large part of the Hindu population has been groaning.
>
> I should be guilty of a breach of trust if I did not warn fellow reformers and caste Hindus in general that the breaking of the fast carried with it a sure promise of a resumption of it if this reform is not relentlessly pursued and achieved within a measurable period.[44]

Four days later, in a letter to his close friend Charlie Andrews, Gandhi said:

> *30 Sept. 1932*: I did expect a mighty response from the orthodox, but I was unprepared for the sudden manifestation that took place. But I shall not be deceived. It remains to be seen whether the temples opened remain open and the various other things done persist.[45]

~

Week after week, Gandhi wrote from prison on the Dalits' condition, and the press published his comments. His reminder to caste Hindus of 'the wrongs we have heaped' on Dalit heads was cuttingly candid:

> Socially they are lepers. Economically they are worse than slaves. Religiously they are denied entrance to places we miscall 'houses of God'. They are denied the use, on the same terms as the caste men, of public roads, public hospitals, public wells, public taps, public parks and the like, and in some cases their approach within a measured distance is a social crime, [or]...their very sight is an offence.
>
> They are relegated for their residence to the worst quarters of cities or villages where they practically get no social services. Caste Hindu lawyers and doctors will not serve them... Brahmins will not officiate at their religious functions. The wonder is that they are at all able to eke out an existence or that they still remain within the Hindu fold. They are too downtrodden to rise in revolt against their suppressors.[46]

~

The Empire's conduct in 1932 contained a welcome oddity. While suppressing the freedom movement and keeping Gandhi and many others in jail, the Empire nonetheless permitted him to edit from his prison cell the English-language journal *Harijan*, which he launched in February 1933, and which was soon accompanied by the Gujarati

Harijanbandhu ('Brother to Harijans'), and the Hindi *Harijan Sevak* ('Servant of Harijans').

From September 1932, Gandhi had started calling the untouchables 'Harijans' (People of God), a phrase first proposed in 1931 by an untouchable reader of Gandhi's journal *Navajivan*,[47] who cited that usage by Gujarat's fifteenth-century saint-poet, Narsi Mehta, the creator of the *Vaishnava Jana* song. Calling himself a 'self-chosen Harijan', Gandhi wrote on 28 April 1933:

> The term has not been coined with a view to perpetuating the separate identity of Harijans... The term 'untouchable' savours of contempt... [I]n so far as untouchables have a distinct identity, we must have a name by which to call them... Let us pray that this separateness may be done away with so that all of us may become fit to be called 'Harijans'—men of God. (*Harijan Sevak*, 28 April 1933)[48]

Ambedkar disliked the 'Harijan' phrase and continued to distance himself from Gandhi. Declining Gandhi's request for 'a message' from him for the opening issue of *Harijan*, he however sent a 'statement' where he said that nothing short of 'the destruction of the caste system' could finish untouchability. Outcastes existed, Ambedkar wrote, because there were castes. He also indicated a desire to leave the Hindu fold.

Unwilling as yet to denounce the caste system as such, Gandhi linked untouchability not to the existence of castes but to a tragic acceptance of the notion of high and low. On 14 February 1933, he wrote:

> If this doctrine of utmost superiority and utmost inferiority, descending from father to son for eternity, is an integral part of Hinduism...then I no more want to belong to it than does Dr Ambedkar. But...there is no superiority or inferiority in the Hinduism of my conception.
>
> I invite Dr Ambedkar to shed his bitterness and anger and try to learn the beauties of the faith of his forefathers. Let him not curse Hinduism without making an unbiased study of it, and if it fails to sustain him in his hour of need, by all means let him forsake it.[49]

Ambedkar was not persuaded. Although the Congress had thus far shunned the weak central legislature set up by the Raj, Gandhi blessed two bills moved there by an elected member, Ranga Iyer, one seeking to prohibit discrimination against Dalits, the other making it unlawful for an orthodox minority to bar Dalits from entering a temple. The second bill arose from the failure of a reformist majority of worshippers at Kerala's famed Guruvayur temple to have the temple opened to Dalits.

Fellow prisoner Vallabhbhai Patel pointed out to Gandhi that while a man like Malaviya had opposed Ranga

Iyer's bills, Ambedkar had claimed that the Dalits did not really care about temple entry. Patel's advice to Gandhi was to 'let the two parties quarrel', not allow himself 'to come between' the two. Disagreeing, Gandhi told Patel that Dalits could not be allowed to 'feel that they have been left to their fate' (16 February 1933).[50]

Bowing to orthodox pressure, Ranga Iyer withdrew his Bills, and there were ugly demonstrations by purist sanatanists against Gandhi. One of Gandhi's oldest friends, Ranchhoddas Patwari, demanded (and received) precise replies to eighty-eight questions; he predicted that Gandhi's stand against orthodoxy would wreck the Congress, and suggested that Gandhi had 'completely forsaken dharma'. One of Patwari's questions was whether Gandhi's parents would have approved of Dalits entering temples. 'No,' replied Gandhi.[51]

However, Hindus wanting reform felt Gandhi to be their champion. So did a great many Dalits. Gandhi seemed confident that the bulk of the Hindu community would follow him, isolating the purists. To Nehru, who was in prison, he wrote:

> *15 Feb. 1933*: The fight against sanatanists is becoming more and more interesting if also increasingly difficult... The abuses they are hurling at me are wonderfully refreshing. I am all that is bad and corrupt on this earth. But the storm will subside... [I]t is the death dance of the moth around a lamp.[52]

In May 1933, Gandhi consolidated his position through a fresh fast—this time, he claimed, 'a self-purificatory' one—for twenty-one days. The previous fast had put pressure on orthodoxy and also on Ambedkar. Now, making no demands on anyone, he would put pressure only on himself. He wrote:

> The evil [of untouchability] is far greater than even I had thought it to be. It will not be eradicated by money, external organization and even political power for Harijans, though all these three are necessary. But to be effective, they must follow or at least accompany...inward power... This can only come by fasting and prayer.[53]

On the night of 8 May, some hours after the fast began, not wishing to risk his death in custody, the Empire released Gandhi. Coming out, Gandhi asked M.S. Aney, the acting Congress president, to announce a six-week suspension of the disobedience campaign, which had continued even though most leaders were in jail.

This chronology reveals the positive interconnection between the two struggles, one against untouchability and the other against British rule. When repression made defiance of British rule unbearably costly, the fight against untouchability, essential in its own right, became a surrogate struggle for independence, and one which the Empire could not possibly oppose.

Breadwinners had gone to prison for long periods in 1930 and 1932. Many were still inside. Donations to the Congress were banned, and its funds seized or dried up. As Gandhi would say in a letter to Andrews, Viceroy Lord Willingdon's ordinance rule had 'struck the people dumb'. The masses were 'terror-struck' and 'the well-to-do' were 'trembling in their shoes' through fear of the Raj. 'And so there is a kind of dead calm which even in my bed, isolated though I am from contact with people through the orders of doctors, I can't help sensing.' (15 June 1933)[54]

But Gandhi was not giving up. He claimed, in this letter to Andrews, that 'time...counts in our favour', and there was 'a certainty of the final triumph'. Andrews had asked Gandhi to concentrate on untouchability removal 'for the whole remainder of your life, without turning to the right or the left'. Recalling that Gandhi had 'again and again' said that with untouchability Indians were 'not fit' for Swaraj, Andrews asked his friend not to try 'to serve two masters'.[55]

This was similar to what Ambedkar too had urged, but Gandhi turned down the advice.

> *To Andrews, 15 June 1933*: Now for your important argument about untouchability. But there is this initial flaw about it. My life is one indivisible whole. It is not built after the compartmental system—satyagraha, civil resistance, untouchability, Hindu-Muslim unity...are indivisible parts of a whole...

> You will find at one time in my life an emphasis on one thing, at another time on other. But that is just like a pianist, now emphasizing one note and now other. But they are all related to one another.
>
> Therefore you see how it is utterly impossible for me to say: 'I have now nothing to do with civil disobedience or Swaraj!' Not only so... Full and final removal of untouchability...is utterly impossible without Swaraj... Love. Mohan[56]

~

As to how to work for Swaraj, Gandhi modified his strategy. During two conversations held in Pune on 1 and 2 June 1933, Gandhi and acting Congress president Rajagopalachari agreed that the current round of mass struggle should come to an end. It was a conclusion that Gandhi and Patel had already if privately reached behind Yerawada's walls. Deliberating in Pune in Gandhi's presence, Congress leaders who were free endorsed the new approach.

The new thinking had been encouraged by HMG's White Paper of March 1933 on political reform in India, which offered wide powers to elected provincial legislatures and also contemplated a new federal assembly where the princes or their nominees would fill a third of the seats.

Gandhi could not countenance any major role by hereditary princes in a federal assembly, but provincial power merited a look. Although provincial ministries under the projected scheme would be circumscribed by reserve powers vested in the Viceroy and the governor, these provincial ministries might be able, among other things, to restore lands that officials under British governors had seized from freedom-fighters—and help in a future fight for Swaraj.

As he mulled new strategies, Gandhi moved in September 1933 to Wardha, near Nagpur. Situated near the eastern end of the Marathi country, Wardha was close to India's geographical centre and was the town of the businessman-industrialist Jamnalal Bajaj, Gandhi's enthusiastic backer.

~

In November, after he had gained strength, Gandhi, now sixty-four, began another all-India tour, this time with an exclusive focus against untouchability.

It was an unprecedented campaign. His wife Kasturba, Mahadev Desai, Pyarelal and other close companions were still in jail, but new colleagues travelled with Gandhi. Between November 1933 and March 1934, Gandhi and his team visited Nagpur and the Vidarbha area of the Marathi country; Bilaspur and the large tribal tract of Chhattisgarh; the Hindi-speaking Mahakoshal region of central India; Bhopal and Delhi and places adjacent; Vijayawada and over seventy towns and villages in the Telugu country; the Kannada and Malayalam regions; the Tamil country; the

Coorg area; and Mangalore, Belgaum, Bijapur and other places in south-western India.

Everywhere he collected money for the Dalit cause, wrote for his new weeklies, visited the quarters where Dalits lived, sought their entry into temples, and insisted that anyone welcoming him in a town or village should describe the condition of its Dalits. And he spoke frankly:

> 'If my taking up that position [of attacking untouchability] results in weakening Hinduism,' he said on 18 January 1934, in Alleppey, 'I cannot help it... I want to exorcize the devil of untouchability.[57]

After a huge earthquake destroyed towns and villages in north Bihar (15 January 1934), Gandhi sought money for Bihar as well, but he refused, despite urgings by some, to divert funds collected for Dalits to earthquake relief. Also, he controversially suggested that the earthquake was 'a divine chastisement' for 'the great sin' committed for centuries by the so-called higher castes against Dalits, a 'calamity handed down...from century to century'.[58]

Criticizing Gandhi's 'superstitious' argument, Tagore said that the logic 'far better suits the psychology of [Gandhi's] opponents than his own', and that the orthodox were likely to 'hold [Gandhi] and his followers responsible for the visitation of Divine anger'.[59] But Gandhi could not resist using the earthquake to drive home the iniquity of untouchability.

> '[W]hilst we have yet breathing time', he said on 24 January, 'let us get rid of the distinctions of high and low, purify our hearts, and be ready to face our Maker when an earthquake or some natural calamity or death in the ordinary course overtakes us.'[60]

In March and April, Gandhi spent more than four weeks in Bihar's devastated areas, consoling victims and supporting relief work, and again linked the calamity to untouchability. There were angry protests from sanatanists, who came with black flags to his meetings. These drew immense and supportive crowds, as his meetings in southern and central India had done. He interpreted the enthusiastic response as a sign that 'untouchability has become weak and limp'.[61]

Orthodoxy was not content with raising flags and slogans. In April 1934, the car he had entered after arriving at Jasidih train station in Bihar was angrily stoned and smashed, but Gandhi survived the attack.[62] A couple of months later, on 24 June 1934, in Pune, Gandhi said that Dalits prevented from drawing water from public wells should, if necessary, seek protection from the police and courts of law.[63] Two days after he had said this, an assailant threw a bomb at a car thought to be carrying Gandhi. Occupants were injured but Gandhi was in another car. The bomb-thrower in Pune was not caught or identified. Whether he had links to those who would kill Gandhi in 1948 is not known.

~

Shortly before Gandhi's Pune visit, Ambedkar had met him in Mumbai and related incidents of maltreatment of Dalits, whereupon Gandhi requested Ambedkar to send him 'full facts' about every such occurrence.[64] In July, Gandhi lauded Ambedkar in a public speech in Karachi:

> The magnitude of his sacrifice is great... He leads a simple life. He is also in a position to settle down in Europe if he so desires. But he doesn't want to stay there. He is only concerned about the welfare of the Harijans. But even a man like him [finds] that no Hindu family in Pune would accept him as a colleague or a friend.[65]

Ambedkar was embarked on his own far-reaching journey. In 1935, he was appointed principal of the Government Law College in Mumbai, and became a professor there as well, positions he would occupy for two years. In May 1935, his wife Ramabai died after a long illness. She had wanted to make a pilgrimage to Pandharpur, but her husband had not allowed it, for as an untouchable she would not have been permitted to enter its famed temple.[66]

In August 1935, when untouchables in Gujarat's Kavitha village, about 20 kilometres south of Ahmedabad, sent four of their children to the village school, there was a hostile reaction from Kavitha's caste Hindus, who withdrew their children from the 'polluted' school. A Dalit in the village was assaulted. When Dalit males went to nearby Dholka to file a criminal complaint, Kavitha's Dalit quarter was attacked by a crowd that included women. The caste Hindus refused to hire Kavitha's Dalits as labourers, or sell them foodstuffs, or allow them to graze their cattle. Kerosene was poured into the Dalit well.

Asked by Gandhi to deal with Kavitha's ugly developments, Vallabhbhai Patel, who had been released in July 1934, went to the village and secured an undertaking from caste Hindus that they would cease hurting the Dalits, who withdrew their legal complaint.

Ambedkar was far from satisfied. How would the Dalits enforce the undertaking, he asked?[67]

On 13 October 1935, he presided at a Conversion Conference of the Depressed Classes held in Yeola, about 45 kilometres east of Nashik, where he advised the Depressed Classes to abandon all agitation for temple-entry privileges. Instead, added Ambedkar in a landmark statement, 'they should leave Hinduism entirely and embrace another religion'. He vowed: 'I solemnly assure you that I will not die as a Hindu.'[68] In other remarks in Yeola, Ambedkar said:

> It is an error to look upon religion as a matter which is individual, private and personal... The correct view is that religion, like language, is social... [Each] is essential for social life, and the individual has to have it because without it he cannot participate in the life of the society.
>
> Socially, the Untouchables will gain absolutely and immensely...by conversion [because] the Untouchables

> will be members of a community whose religion has universalized and equalized all values of life. Such a blessing is unthinkable for them while they are in the Hindu fold...
>
> Is there any place in the Hindu society for a convert to the Hindu faith? Now the organisation of the Hindu society is characterized by the existence of castes. Each caste...only allows individuals born in it to its membership and does not allow any one from outside being brought into it. The Hindu Society being a federation of castes, and each caste being self-enclosed, there is no place for the convert, for no caste will admit him...
>
> If the Hindu society desires to survive it must think not of adding to its numbers but increasing its solidarity and that means the abolition of caste.[69]

These views were embodied in a resolution passed by the Yeola conference. Clearly disturbed, Gandhi offered a public response:

> I can understand the anger of a high-souled and highly educated person like Dr Ambedkar over the atrocities as were committed in Kavitha and other villages. But religion is not like a house or a cloak which can be changed at will...
>
> [C]hange of faith by him and those who passed the resolution will not serve the cause which they have at heart; for millions of unsophisticated, illiterate Harijans

> will not listen to him and them...especially when it is remembered that their lives, for good or for evil, are intertwined with those of caste Hindus.[70]

When Ambedkar was shown Gandhi's comment, he replied with these words:

> What religion we shall belong to is not decided; what ways and means we shall adopt, we have not thought out; but we have decided one thing, and that after due deliberation and with deep conviction, that Hindu religion is not good for us.
>
> Inequality is the very basis of it... Let none think I have done this in a huff or as a matter of wrath against the treatment meted out to the Depressed Classes at Kavitha village... It is a deeply deliberated decision. I agree with Gandhiji that religion is necessary, but I do not agree that man should have his ancestral religion if he finds that that religion is repugnant to his notions of the sort of religion he needs.[71]

~

In another response, Gandhi now criticized the caste system directly. Thus far, in order to show his Hindu loyalty, Gandhi had defended an idealized caste system, the so-called *varnashrama dharma*, with his own definition of that phrase. He interpreted the *varnashrama* system as a division of occupations based on aptitude and as an arrangement that rejected inequalities, while freely conceding that such a picture did not exist on the ground.

He had offered this fanciful picture as a sop to fellow caste Hindus, and in order to sugar-coat the bitter pill of anti-untouchability. After Ambedkar's Yeola declaration, Gandhi came out with language that was earthier and clearer. In an article in *Harijan* on 16 November 1935, he said of the caste system, 'The sooner public opinion abolishes it, the better.' The article carried the headline, 'CASTE HAS TO GO'. 'Nothing in the Shastras which is manifestly contrary to universal truths and morals can stand', Gandhi added.[72]

Soon, Gandhi was openly espousing inter-dining and intermarriage between caste Hindus and Dalits. On 19 January 1936, *Harijanbandhu*, the Gujarati counterpart of *Harijan*, carried an article where Gandhi wrote of 'unnatural and meaningless restrictions on intermarriage and inter-dining', adding, 'And that is why the country has stopped progressing.'[73]

As for Ambedkar, although eagerly approached by Christian, Muslim and Sikh missionaries, he seemed in no hurry to choose a new religion.

~

In December 1935, Ambedkar was invited by the Jat-Pat-Todak Mandal, a Lahore-based body of reformist Hindus, to preside over its annual conference scheduled for the following spring. Accepting the invitation, Ambedkar gave much thought and time to prepare his presidential lecture. Whether or not he knew that he was composing a text that would become an instant classic and, later, influence Indians generation after generation, a text, moreover, that scholars the world over would pore over, it seems clear to anyone reading *The Annihilation of Caste*, as he titled his lecture, that Ambedkar had put all of his mind and soul into it.

It was not enough, Ambedkar declared in the lecture, to defy caste. The religious texts that justified it, the Shastras, had to be opposed too. If asked, 'What is your ideal society if you do not want caste?' he would say, Ambedkar wrote, 'a society based on *Liberty, Equality, and Fraternity*. And why not?'

Urging reformers to confront Hindu society's ills in the frankest manner possible, Ambedkar ended the lecture by alluding to his own decision to leave the Hindu fold. 'I am sorry, I will not be with you,' he said. 'I have decided to change. This is not the place for giving reasons. But even when I am gone out of your fold, I will watch your movement with active sympathy, and you will have my assistance for what it may be worth.'

'Yours is a national cause,' he concluded, and one 'more difficult than the other national cause, namely Swaraj. In the fight for Swaraj you fight with the whole nation on your side. In this, you have to fight against the whole nation—and that too, your own. But it is more important than Swaraj.'[74]

It is noteworthy that Ambedkar and Gandhi both felt that ending Indian society's sin was more important than Swaraj.

After the Jat-Pat-Todak Mandal's leaders read Ambedkar's text (and after Ambedkar had printed copies of it in Mumbai), they pleaded with Ambedkar to revise it. The Mandal's supporters would be offended, he was told, by his remarks in condemnation of the Shastras and about leaving the Hindu fold.

When Ambedkar expressed inability to rewrite as urged, the conference was cancelled, which only heightened interest in the contents of *Annihilation of Caste*. And when, in two successive issues of *Harijan* in July 1936, Gandhi critiqued the text, while praising much of it, not only was this interest further magnified; in a rejoinder, Ambedkar took the opportunity to puncture Gandhi's purely theoretical portrayal of Hindu society's contented and equal *varnas* performing their hereditary tasks.

~

In 1941, a year after the Muslim League, led by Jinnah, had asked for the separation from India of Muslim-majority areas, Ambedkar published his *Pakistan or the Partition of India*. Containing as it did a solid analysis of the pros and cons of the League's Pakistan demand, *Pakistan or the Partition of India* was cited by both Gandhi and Jinnah during their extensive yet unsuccessful negotiations in Mumbai in September 1944.[75]

Commenting in his book on Jinnah's anxieties about a Hindu Raj, Ambedkar wrote: 'If Hindu Raj does become a fact, it will, no doubt, be the greatest calamity for this country... Hindu Raj must be prevented at any cost.'

However, Ambedkar doubted that Pakistan was 'the true remedy against' Hindu Raj, and he expressed disappointment that Jinnah had not worked to create an all-India alliance, in opposition to the INC, of Muslims, Dalits and non-Brahmin caste Hindus. Despite such remarks, Ambedkar said in *Pakistan or the Partition of India*: 'I hold firmly that...if the Musalmans are bent on having Pakistan, then it must be conceded to them.'[76]

Why the 1947 Partition happened is a question outside the scope of this study of fraternity in the context of India's Constitution and its making. We can, however, mark that the carnage that accompanied Partition underlined what the absence of fraternity can do. That carnage also made restoring fraternity both essential and difficult.

In 1942, a year after Ambedkar published *Pakistan or the Partition of India*, he accepted an invitation from the Viceroy to join his executive council as Member for Labour, a position Ambedkar occupied until June 1946. In 1942, on his part, Gandhi launched Quit India. Once more, in common with tens of thousands of activists, Gandhi found himself in jail, in his case again in Pune. He was released after two years.

In 1945, a year after the abortive Gandhi–Jinnah talks, Ambedkar published the book previously mentioned, *What Congress and Gandhi Have Done to the Untouchables,* which contained scalding attacks on Gandhi and the Congress. However, along with Partition, independence was approaching, and on 9 December 1946, a Constituent Assembly, its members chosen by provincial legislatures formed by elections held during the 1945–46 winter, held its first sitting.

Ambedkar was one of its members, elected to it by the legislature of what was still the undivided province of Bengal, which had a Muslim majority and a Muslim League ministry. Jinnah, the League's all-India chief, had backed Ambedkar's election from Bengal. Although, as part of its strategy for achieving Partition, the Muslim League boycotted the Constituent Assembly's sessions, Ambedkar chose to attend them, a decision publicly commended in February 1947 by Gandhi, who was then in Noakhali in eastern Bengal.[77]

By this time Ambedkar had heard in Mumbai from one of Gandhi's British associates, Muriel Lester, that in view of Dr Ambedkar's learning and leadership, Gandhi wanted the Congress to include him in free India's central cabinet. After Lester gave Gandhi an account of Ambedkar's positive reaction, Gandhi asked Nehru and Patel to invite him.[78]

Starting with Prime Minister Jawaharlal Nehru and Deputy Prime Minister Vallabhbhai Patel, the names of the ministers in free India's first cabinet may be viewed as a poster for fraternity. The list of fourteen included two Dalits (Ambedkar and Jagjivan Ram), two Muslims (Abul Kalam Azad and Rafi Ahmed Kidwai), two Christians (John Matthai and Amrit Kaur), a Sikh (Baldev Singh), and a Parsi (C.H. Bhabha), but only one woman (Amrit Kaur).

Ambedkar was the Minister for Law. On 29 August, two weeks after Independence, the Constituent Assembly—which was the body to which power over India was transferred from HMG in London—appointed Ambedkar as the Chairman of its Drafting Committee. More than two years later, on 25 November 1949, when the Constitution steered by him was being adopted, Ambedkar said:

> I came into the Constituent Assembly with no greater aspiration than to safeguard the interests of the Scheduled Castes. I had not the remotest idea that I would be called upon to undertake more responsible functions. I was therefore greatly surprised when the Assembly elected me to the Drafting Committee. I was more than surprised when the Drafting Committee elected me to be its Chairman.[79]

Safeguarding the interests of the Scheduled Castes was a mighty commitment. Everyone knows that Ambedkar discharged that pledge—and didn't stop with that.

~

Nine months before Independence, on 13 December 1946, Nehru had moved in the Constituent Assembly the 'Objectives Resolution'. Passed on 22 January 1947, this resolution, which would supply the basis for our Constitution's Preamble, sought to establish a sovereign republic

- where 'all power and authority of independent India, its constituent parts and organs of government, *are derived from the people*';
- where 'shall be guaranteed and secured to all the people of India *justice, social, economic, and political; equality of status, of opportunity, and before the law; freedom of thought, expression, belief, faith, worship, vocation, association and action*, subject to law and public morality';
- where 'adequate safeguards shall be provided for minorities, backward and tribal areas, and depressed and other backward classes';
- and where '*the integrity* of the territory of the Republic and its sovereign rights on land, sea and

air' shall be maintained 'according to justice and the law of civilized nations';

- enabling 'this ancient land [to] attain its rightful and honoured place in the world and make its full and willing contribution to the promotion of world peace and the welfare of mankind'.

The similarities between the foregoing and the eventual Preamble to the Constitution are impossible to miss:

> *We, the people of India,* having solemnly resolved to constitute India into a sovereign socialist secular democratic republic and to secure to all its citizens: *justice, social, economic and political; liberty of thought, expression, belief, faith and worship; equality of status and of opportunity*; and to promote among them all fraternity assuring the dignity of the individual and *the unity* and integrity of the nation; in our Constituent Assembly this twenty-sixth day of November, 1949, do hereby adopt, enact and give to ourselves this Constitution.

A conspicuous difference between these two short texts is that the Objectives Resolution does not include the word 'fraternity'. The history of the inclusion of 'fraternity' in the Preamble is not hard to capture.

We saw how Ambedkar wrote in *Annihilation of Caste* in 1935–36 that his 'ideal society' would be 'based on Liberty, Equality, and Fraternity'. Twelve years later, on

21 February 1948, writing as the Chairman of the Constituent Assembly's Drafting Committee to Rajendra Prasad (the Assembly's president), Ambedkar said:

> The Committee has added a clause about fraternity in the preamble, although it does not occur in the Objectives Resolution. The committee felt that the need for fraternal concord and goodwill in India was never greater than now and that this particular aim of the new Constitution should be emphasized by special mention in the preamble.[80]

The volumes entitled *The Framing of India's Constitution: Select Documents*, edited by B. Shiva Rao and available online, contain much information about the Drafting Committee's work. Page 484 of Volume III of this series, providing minutes of the Drafting Committee's meeting of 6 February 1948 and reproducing the draft preamble, contains the word 'fraternity'.

We may safely infer from the 6 February date that the inclusion of 'fraternity' was prompted by the assassination of Mahatma Gandhi, which had occurred a week earlier.

Two years or so later, in his famous speech of 25 November 1949 to the Constituent Assembly, Ambedkar would say what we have previously quoted: 'Without fraternity, equality and liberty will be no deeper than coats of paint.' We should look at more of this speech.

> Political democracy cannot last unless there lies at the base of it social democracy. What does social democracy mean? It means a way of life which recognizes liberty, equality and fraternity as the principles of life... These principles of liberty, equality and fraternity are not to be treated as separate items in a trinity. They form a union... [T]o divorce one from the other is to defeat the very purpose of democracy.
>
> Liberty cannot be divorced from equality. Equality cannot be divorced from liberty. Nor can liberty and equality be divorced from fraternity. Without equality, liberty would produce the supremacy of the few over the many. Equality without liberty would kill individual initiative.
>
> Without fraternity, liberty would produce the supremacy of the few over the many. Without fraternity, liberty and equality could not become a natural course of things. It would require a constable to enforce them...
>
> What does fraternity mean? Fraternity means a sense of common brotherhood of all Indians—of Indians being one people. It is the principle which gives unity and solidarity to social life.[81]

As relevant in the third decade of the twenty-first century as they were in 1949, these remarks by Ambedkar are a fresh reminder that human rights or fundamental rights are not merely a matter between the people and a government. They are connected to how we as a people treat one another. A constitutional and a political principle, fraternity is a human need too.

To explore fraternity's fuller meaning, let us return to its place in the Preamble, which highlights, as was noted in the opening chapter, two crucial purposes of fraternity. According to the Preamble, 'We, the people of India' have 'solemnly resolved to promote among all citizens *fraternity*, assuring the *dignity* of the individual and *the unity and integrity* of the nation'.

Let's not miss the deep import of this sentence. By requiring us to esteem each fellow citizen, fraternity assures the individual's dignity or self-respect. Moreover, because fraternity requires us to think for, feel for, be considerate towards one another, it assures the nation's unity and integrity. How potent fraternity is!

We cannot be surprised on finding that Gandhi was as keen as Ambedkar on fraternity. Writing in 1945 about the Adivasis—a great and probably foundational component of our nation (a people whom, regrettably, this short book has not even begun to address)—Gandhi said:

> Our country is so vast and the races so varied that the best of us cannot know all there is to know of men and their condition. As one discovers this for oneself, one realizes how difficult it is to make good our claim to be one nation, unless every unit has a living consciousness of being one with every other.[82]

'A living consciousness of being one with every other individual' would be a pretty good definition of fraternity, and it is not hard to see why such a realization would strengthen a nation's unity and integrity.

We may digress here for a moment to mark that modern European political scientists and critical theorists have acknowledged the significance of fraternity. Holding that 'struggle for recognition' is what 'best characterizes the fight for emancipation by social groups', these theorists see 'the notion of fraternity' in a historical line that runs from the French Revolution to our times. In the 1990s, for example, communities in the Balkans demanded recognition through gory conflicts, obliging European scholars to remember fraternity.[83]

~

During independent India's opening six months, as Ambedkar worked on a Constitution that would guide future ministers, legislators, judges, bureaucrats, policemen and soldiers, Gandhi continued his struggle to bring all the Indian people closer to one another. He had failed to avert Partition, yet India was finally free. Free from rule by a distant power yet engulfed by fires of hatred.

Going directly to the people—in West Bengal, Bihar, Delhi and the portion of East Punjab that would later become Haryana—Gandhi doused the deadly flames. In

Harsh Mander's words, 'The Mahatma in these last months of his life, showed us the power of radical, fearless love. He also lit our way to a secular, just and kind India of the future, an India founded on iridescent bonds of fraternity.'[84]

He did other essential things before his assassination on 30 January 1948. He ensured a sufficient degree of unity among his freedom-struggle lieutenants who had become the country's political rulers: Nehru and Patel in particular, but also Azad, Rajaji and Rajendra Prasad (and others). He kept reminding the Congress party and its representatives in the Constituent Assembly (which also served as the nation's parliament between August 1947 and January 1950) of their pledges to establish a state that was religiously neutral and socially pro-poor. And he kept reminding the leaders and the people of their solemn pledges against untouchability.

In that year of independence, even as some on the subcontinent fell into inhumanity, a larger number did not. They must be saluted. Bravely protecting vulnerable fellow humans, they assisted treks to safety across the new border. If Gandhi's two fasts in aid of the subcontinent's minorities, one undertaken in Kolkata in September 1947 and the other in Delhi in January 1948, awakened feelings of humanity and stemmed the tide of madness, the role of the unknown soldier for fraternity was just as crucial. On 2 November 1947, Gandhi related what one such individual was doing in Lahore:

> A wonderful thing I [have] learnt about Lahore is that a Muslim gentleman has kept a Sikh in his own house [and has] kept a copy of the Guru Granth Saheb in one of the rooms of the house with due respect. He has saved that Sikh because he happens to be his friend. This makes me very happy.[85]

~

Babasaheb Ambedkar would live until the night of 5–6 December 1956, when, at the age of 65, he died in Delhi. Disappointed at the pace of the legislation introduced by him for reforming Hindu society, he had resigned from the Indian cabinet in September 1951. In 1954, ending the suspense that had lingered since 1935, he announced that he would embrace Buddhism. Dogged by ill-health but unrelenting in his scholarly toil, he completed *The Buddha and His Dhamma* in March 1956.

On 14 October 1956, in Nagpur, he formally converted to Buddhism, a step in which he was joined by tens of thousands of Dalits at the time and later by hundreds of thousands. On 2 December, just three days before his death, this phenomenal warrior-lawmaker-thinker completed the manuscript of his last finished work, *The Buddha or Karl Marx*, and gave it for typing.

~

Justice and solidarity in Indian society were what a great many besides Ambedkar and Gandhi also worked for in the last century. In the South, caste arrogance had received deadly hits from the Malayalam country's social and spiritual leader, Narayana Guru (1856–1928), and from the father of the Dravidian movement, Periyar Ramaswamy (1879–1973). The words of these two, proclaiming the unity of humanity and rejecting absurd hierarchies, possessed irrefutable logic. The two also left behind organizations to propagate their thinking.

Uttered before the Congress plenary of 1940, over which he presided, Abul Kalam Azad's unforgettable words at Ramgarh continue to sing of fraternity among all Indians:

> I am proud of being an Indian. I am a part of the indivisible unity that is Indian nationality. I am indispensable to this noble edifice, and without me this splendid structure of India is incomplete. I am an essential element which has gone to build India. I can never surrender this claim.
>
> Full eleven centuries have passed by since [it first came to India]. Islam has now as great a claim on the soil of India as Hinduism. If Hinduism has been the religion of the people here for several thousands of years, Islam also has been their religion for a thousand years. Just as a Hindu can say with pride that he is an Indian and follows Hinduism, so also we can say with equal pride that we are Indians and follow Islam... The Indian Christian is

> equally entitled to say with pride that he is an Indian and is following a religion of India, namely Christianity.[86]

Was any Indian's passion for Hindu–Muslim–Christian–Sikh unity deeper than what Netaji Subhas Bose nursed in his bosom? That passion was reflected in the plural composition and secular character of the Indian National Army, and in the Urdu motto Bose chose for it: *Ittehad, Ittemad, Qurbani*, or Unity, Faith, Sacrifice. The passion was revealed afresh in the national slogan that Bose bequeathed (a brainchild, it appears, of his close aide, Abid Hasan): *Jai Hind!*[87]

That all Indians belonged to one another was also, we should recall, the uncompromising message of India's beloved young martyr, Bhagat Singh.

There was, too, the role of the steadfast Left. As has been true elsewhere in the world as well, India's Left movements, born in the twentieth century's opening decades, were unable to prevent splits in their ranks. For triggering action and mobilization in India, moreover, caste was proving more useful than class. Nonetheless, Indian society in the last century was goaded in the direction of equality and fraternity by Left and Progressive movements, which many of India's gifted poets, writers and artists had embraced.

Recognizing before most others the latent political power of the oft ignored 'backward castes', Rammanohar Lohia (1910–1967) merged caste and class battles in portions of the country and widened the ground-level appeal of socialism.

And when in the 1970s Prime Minister Indira Gandhi and her younger son Sanjay were tempted to flout democratic requirements, Jayaprakash Narayan, 1942's Quit India's hero, but by this time an elderly socialist, bounced back, bonded once more with the nation's youth, and led a great struggle for human rights.[88]

The 37-year period between the elections of March 1977, when India's voters took the opportunity unexpectedly offered by Indira Gandhi to remove her from office, and the elections of 2014, when Narendra Modi became prime minister for the first time, the country witnessed multiple changes of government and prime ministers. While all these governments were well supplied with flaws, none of them questioned independent India's foundational idea. Embedded, as we have seen, in the Preamble, that idea was that the nation belonged to all Indians. No group identified with any particular religion would be privileged, and no group deprived.

The years from 2014 onwards have seen a departure, at times publicly avowed, at other times unspoken yet unmistakable, from this commitment. Fraternity has been under attack in India.

What about our neighbourhood? That's the subject of the next chapter.

Chapter V

Know Thy Neighbour

In another short book recently written by me,[89] I made an observation that may be relevant to what we've been discussing in this study:

> 'To think of fellow Indians in religious, linguistic, or caste terms', I wrote, 'has become a habit with us. Is it impossible to see [fellow Indians] as neighbours? India has 80 percent Hindus, 14 or 15 percent Muslims, 2½ percent Christians—and 100 percent neighbours.'

All Indians are neighbours to one another. Isn't that our common identity, shared without exception by all of us? The portion of Planet Earth that we call South Asia is, likewise, a neighbourhood. We in India may see Nepal as a Hindu land, Bhutan, Myanmar and Sri Lanka as chiefly Buddhist nations, and Pakistan, Bangladesh, Afghanistan and the Maldives as overwhelmingly Muslim countries. The truth in such a view does not alter the fact that each of these nations is also our immediate, or almost immediate, neighbour.

Absorbing this fact, we may safely say that fraternity's difficult mantra, whether in respect of individuals within a nation or between nations, is 'Love thy neighbour as thyself'.

For any country seeking to protect itself in our fickle and oft-dangerous world, the surest defence, it has sometimes been said, is the friendship and respect of an immediate neighbour. In confirmation of this maxim, we can think of Canada's strong relationship, both government-to-government and people-to-people, with the US. It has saved the latter from immense anxieties and costs. The friendly tie is in fact a huge blessing to both countries.

Here we may recall Article 51 of our Constitution, which spells out a Directive Principle for State Policy. This Article instructs that 'The State shall endeavour to

(a) promote international peace and security;
(b) maintain just and honourable relations between nations;
(c) foster respect for international law and treaty obligations in the dealings of organized peoples with one another; and encourage settlement of international disputes by arbitration.'

~

Many years back, in 1969, i.e. well before Afghanistan entered its seemingly unending era of brutal suffering, before Burma became Myanmar, and when Sri Lanka was still Ceylon, I heard Vinoba Bhave speak in Wardha, Maharashtra, of the desirability of befriending what he called the 'ABC' lands. Vinoba was addressing a public meeting along with two other remarkable figures, Khan Abdul Ghaffar Khan and Jayaprakash Narayan.

Affectionately called Bacha Khan or Badshah Khan by his fellow Pathans (whom we call Pashtuns today), Ghaffar Khan was making a rare visit to India after the 1947 Partition, which, along with Gandhi, he had striven hard but unsuccessfully to prevent. Welcoming this Frontier Gandhi in 1969, Vinoba used the chance to speak of India's need to cultivate friendly relations with Afghanistan, Burma and Ceylon—the 'ABC arc', as Vinoba termed it.

More than half a century later, can anyone declare that India enjoys close-and-warm relations with any of our South Asian neighbours, whether within the ABC arc or beyond it? Government-to-government relations with these neighbours stretch from being minimal, strictly formal, cold and suspicious, which is the case with Pakistan and Afghanistan, to fluctuating, calculated and provisional, which seems to be the case with Nepal, Sri Lanka and Myanmar.

In post-1947 history, people-to-people contacts between

India and Pakistan rarely assumed any large scale. Until about fifteen years ago, however, such contacts were at least enthusiastic and fairly frequent. Visits across the border have now evaporated. Visas seem much harder to obtain and are probably not even being sought in large numbers.

As between India and Bangladesh (which supplied a fresh 'B' to our neighbourhood two years after Vinoba's 1969 remark), official relations have been cordial for quite some time. However, any impression of a strong or deep-rooted partnership is more than cancelled by crude rhetoric in India, at times from high quarters, about Bangladeshis allegedly infiltrating themselves in large numbers into India, and by talk within Bangladesh's population of pressures allegedly applied on Dhaka by New Delhi.

The ranks have certainly thinned of those such as this writer who can remember a time when a name like Chittagong, Dhaka, Karachi, Lahore or Peshawar aroused curiosities and wishes no different from what residents of say Bengaluru or Hyderabad might today imagine when, for example, Jaipur or Patna enters their thoughts.

We have allowed political borders to swallow the mental spaces where our knowledge of pre-1947 realities was stored, and we have allowed those borders to turn into thick high walls.

Stories and songs that in the not so distant past were common to the entire area which in 1947 became India,

Pakistan and Bangladesh have been allowed to disappear. Or they have been banished. Someone like the poet Iqbal is going out of India's textbooks. I suppose '*Saare jahaan se achchha*' will be expunged as well.

We may wonder whether SAARC will remain with us even as a lifeless acronym. There is little to celebrate in SAARC's virtual death. (Those in the current generation who may not even have heard of it should know that SAARC, founded in 1985, stands for the South Asian Association for Regional Cooperation.)

Studying our South Asian neighbourhood can in fact teach us a lot. We can learn, for one thing, that a religious ideology does *not* unite a nation.

Not too long after it was created, 'Islamic' Pakistan broke conspicuously into two pieces. How religion today is 'uniting' or 'strengthening' the half that continued after 1971 to be called Pakistan is one of our world's most instructive stories, if also a deeply tragic one.

That country is being drained by a profusion of internal wars. Wars between parties and within parties. Wars between political parties and the army. Wars between regions and within regions. Between extremist groups and the army. Within extremist groups, between religious groups, inside religious groups, and elsewhere.

With every warring group in Pakistan claiming religious sanction and quoting sacred texts, these wars take place even as galloping inflation, floods and other natural disasters multiply the hardships of the country's millions.

And what has a religious ideology done for Afghanistan? It's a horror story. That landlocked nation, successful in the past in keeping at bay two empires, the Russian and the British, and recently successful in ousting the Americans, is now, under the influence of a religious ideology, locking down the dreams of half its population.

Should we be proud that the suffering of Afghanistan's women fails to disturb us in India? Let me return to Badshah Khan, whose 1969 visit to India was mentioned earlier. I knew him from the year 1945, when I was ten. Along with his older brother, Dr Khan Sahib, who twice became the premier of the Frontier Province, Badshah Khan was staying for some days in what then was our family's New Delhi flat. Fourteen years prior to that, in July 1931 (before I was born), Badshah Khan had hosted my father, Devadas Gandhi, in the Frontier Province.

I last saw Badshah Khan in Mumbai in 1987, a year before his death. Encouraged by some of his followers and by his family, I wrote his biography, which came out in 2004.

Can I forget that after Badshah Khan died in Peshawar in 1988, at the age of 98, he was buried, in obedience to his instructions, in Jalalabad, in Afghanistan? Not just anywhere in Afghanistan but on grounds where he had wished to build a school for orphaned and destitute girls? With this knowledge, can I suppress a longing to see a modicum of women's rights restored in Afghanistan?

Badshah Khan *never* agreed that an Islamic state could solve Pakistan's or Afghanistan's problems. And Gandhi, Ambedkar, Nehru, Patel, Subhas Bose, Rajaji, Rajendra Prasad, Vinoba, Jayaprakash and their colleagues *never* thought that a Hindu state would solve India's problems.

Yet there were those who from the start wished to Hinduize the Indian state. Underlining the fact that neighbouring Nepal seemed to be a Hindu kingdom, these men also believed that a Hindu ideology would produce a flourishing partnership between India and Nepal. Not only would time prove them wrong, Indians have realized that nothing seems to damage a party or politician in Nepal more than a pro-India image.

Reacting to a mural in New Delhi's new parliament building where places in Nepal are evidently marked within Ashoka's ancient empire, some in Kathmandu waged, in the summer of 2023, a 'map war' against India. They showed parts of Bengal, Uttarakhand and Himachal Pradesh, besides Sikkim, within Greater Nepal.[90]

Indians have also found that few rights are defended as stoutly in Nepal as the right to make deals with China for development or trade.

The picture from South Asia's Buddhist-majority lands, Myanmar and Sri Lanka, is not bright either. In fact, vocal sections of the Buddhist clergy in Myanmar and Sri Lanka seem determined not to allow South Asia's Islamist or Hinduist platforms to steal a march over them in hate speech or in promoting majority victimhood.

To their honour, a few of Myanmar's Buddhist monks have bravely protested the suppressions imposed by their country's junta. Still, no one can now be found claiming that 'Buddhist' politics will heal either Myanmar or Sri Lanka.

In Sri Lanka, Buddhist nationalism is being mocked for lately targeting the country's Christians after having earlier demonized the island's Tamils and Muslims, in that order.

Anyone thinking that Hindu nationalism or Hindutva politics can hold India together is therefore betting against logic, history and against contemporary experience around us. With time we may also discover that targeting Muslims or Christians is not enough to create excitement. Scapegoating rival Hindutva groups may seem a more promising tactic.

Not religious politics but the steady march of concern for fellow inhabitants of India, and of South Asia, is what is likely to make a difference. We can call it fraternity, or fellowship, or friendship, or solidarity, or compassion, or care, or love, whatever. The word used is unimportant. What we know is that a simple act of friendship for a neighbour, or an attitude of caring, takes us forward towards unity and strength.

In 1941, Gandhi asked every worker in the freedom movement to identify 'with every one of the millions' living in India, and for doing so to 'cultivate personal friendship with persons representing faiths other than his own'.[91]

More than eighty years later, we must ask whether knowledge among us of religious, caste or ethnic groups 'other than our own' has significantly increased. The ability to acquire this knowledge has certainly escalated, and dramatically so. A finger on a phone, or a click on a computer, can in a fraction of a second summon the Other's world. The current or past story of a group 'other than our own', even in a country 'other than our own', will show up, perhaps in a language we know best.

But we have to be curious. We have to touch or click. Or, and this may be even better, we can find a good book about a community 'other than our own'.

Best of all, we can approach one of 'them' in person, and listen, face to face, to their story.

'Know thyself' is a fabulous but insufficient piece of ancient advice. We need to know our neighbours too. In any corner of India or South Asia, a bid to 'know my neighbours', to know their pain, can't do any harm. More likely than not, it would help. It might even heal, unite and strengthen.

Shortly before he died, Dr Ambedkar underlined this quote from the Buddha: '[T]here is suffering everywhere in the world. Ninety percent of mankind is distressed by sorrow. Suffering mankind should be freed from sorrow—this is [our] basic work.'[92]

Chapter VI

Will That Day Come?

Having lingered earlier with some of our Preamble's meaningful words, we should mark the absence from that text of the charged term 'race'. Evoking a bloodline, and all the passions that a bloodline can summon, 'race' is a powerful word. In many a nation, including our own, epics speak of noble, ignoble or cursed races, and often also of a clash between races, clans or bloodlines.

Another emotive word missing in the Preamble is 'religion'. The 'people' in the phrase with which our Preamble begins are not identified with any 'race' or 'religion'. 'We, the people' means all Indians. Each and every Indian is included. Our Preamble does not privilege or downgrade any race, bloodline, religion or belief.

You may belong to any bloodline, or to mingled bloodlines, or you may be unaware of your bloodline. You may have a particular religious belief, no belief, or a mixture of beliefs. None of that alters the state's duty to enable you—and everyone else—to enjoy the liberties mentioned in the Preamble.

Some indeed wanted to introduce 'race' and/or 'religion' into our Constitution. This was the case before Independence, while the Constitution was being discussed, and after it was adopted. And it remains the wish of some today.

In 1939, as the Second World War was about to start, the then chief of the Rashtriya Swayamsevak Sangh, M.S. Golwalkar, expressed such a wish in totally stark language. In a short book entitled *We, or Our Nationhood Defined* (Bharat Publications, Nagpur), Golwalkar began by praising what Hitler and the Nazis had achieved by 1939:

> German pride in their Fatherland...awoke and ran the risk of starting a fresh world-conflagration, in order to establish one, unparalleled, undisputed German Empire over all [their] 'hereditary territory'. This natural and logical aspiration of Germany has almost been fulfilled.[93]

For Golwalkar, the corollary for India was clear:

> Thus applying the modern understanding of 'Nation' to our present conditions, the conclusion is unquestionably forced upon us that in this country, Hindusthan, the Hindu Race with its Hindu Religion, Hindu Culture and Hindu Language, (the natural family of Sanskrit and her off-springs) complete the Nation concept: that,

> in fine, in Hindusthan exists, and must needs exist, the ancient Hindu nation and naught else but the Hindu Nation. All those not belonging to the national i.e. Hindu Race, Religion, Culture and Language, naturally fall out of the pale of real 'National' life.[94]

To Golwalkar and those who thought like him, Muslims, Christians and other non-Hindus were 'foreign elements' or foreign 'races' even if their forebears had lived in India for a long time, even for a thousand years. Golwalkar wrote:

> There are only two courses open to the foreign elements, either to merge themselves in the national race and adopt its culture, or to live at its mercy so long as the national race may allow them to do so and to quit the country at the sweet will of the national race... [T]he foreign races in Hindusthan must either adopt the Hindu culture and language, must learn to respect and hold in reverence Hindu religion, must entertain no idea but those of the glorification of the Hindu race and culture, i.e., of the Hindu nation and must lose their separate existence to merge in the Hindu race, or may stay in the country, wholly subordinated to the Hindu Nation, claiming nothing, deserving no privileges, far less any preferential treatment—not even citizen's rights. There is, at least should be, no other course for them to adopt.[95]

Today, direct or blunt language of this kind may or may not be used in authorized statements or by heads of established organizations. However, such language is frequently employed by vigilantes and at unofficial gatherings. It is fired by a belief that democracy and fraternity are out of date in the twenty-first century, that the supremacy of an imagined or real racial-religious community is a legitimate and necessary goal, and that contempt towards some groups is a desirable attitude.

The fraternity we're discussing is not an unchallenged or secure value in the India of the 2020s.

~

In a significant 2019 article on fraternity on *The India Forum*, Harsh Mander called for 'a huge public debate about what is the floor of human dignity, socially, below which no human being should be allowed to fall'.[96] He went on to say:

> Based on the outcomes of this debate, we should build a new social contract founded on fraternity in new and rapidly growing India. Our contract should be that we will together build a country—and world—in which no child will sleep hungry, no child will sleep under the open sky, no child will be sent to work instead of a school which is as good a school as for any other child her age, no person will be subjected to discrimination or violence because of her identity, no person will be denied free, good-quality healthcare, and no old person will have to work or beg to live with dignity.

> For this to be possible, we first need to reclaim the idea... that we owe it to each other as human beings that we all take care of each other. It requires the kindling of the ideas of solidarity and social caring.

In this article, which I liberally quote from or paraphrase here, Harsh Mander also depicted two contrasting incidents occurring in May and June of 2017, one in the US and the other in India. Both took place on commuter trains. On 26 May 2017, two teenaged young women were shuttling in the metropolitan area of Portland in America's west coast state of Oregon. One girl was Black, the other visibly Muslim, for she wore a hijab. Suddenly, a white man in his thirties with shoulder-length hair, later identified as a member of a white supremacist group, 'racially harangued the two girls'. They did not belong to America and did not pay taxes, he shouted. They 'should go back to Saudi Arabia'.

Three men on the train separately approached the enraged man and formed a protective ring between him and the terrified girls. 'You can't disrespect these young ladies like that,' they said to him. When the girls were getting off the train, they saw the man attacking their protectors with a knife. He slit the throats of two, and savagely sliced into the thigh of the third.

One mortally wounded man, 23-year-old college student Taliesin Namkai-Meche, fell on the floor of the compartment. A few passengers tried desperately to stop his bleeding. 'I am going to die,' he said. As they picked him up, his last words were, 'Tell everyone on the train that I love them.'

The second man whose throat was slit was 53-year-old Rick Best, an air force veteran and father of four. He too died on the platform. The third young man, a poet, 21-year-old Micah Fletcher, survived his injuries in hospital. The three became heroes. It seems, interestingly enough, that Namkai-Meche was raised in a white family influenced by Hindu and Buddhist cultures.[97] One of the girls protected by the three men would later tell a TV channel:

'They didn't even know me. They lost their life because of me and my friend and the way we looked. I just want to say thank you to them and their family... [W]ithout them we probably would be dead right now.'[98]

Less than a month later, on 24 June 2017, in India, again on a commuter train, a Muslim teenager was the target of hate assaults. Along with his brothers Hashim and Shaqir, Junaid Khan was returning to his Haryana village by a local train after they had shopped for Eid in Delhi's walled city. The boys found seats and played Ludo on their phones. At Okhla, where a large crowd got in, Junaid gave his seat to an old man. A group of men demanded that the other brothers also vacate their seats. When they held on, the men abused them racially, asked them to go to Pakistan, and taunted them for being circumcised. They pulled off the young men's skullcaps, tugged at their beards, and thrashed them.

They did not let the brothers get down at their destination. Instead, as the train sped ahead, they took out knives, stabbed the three, and threw them out at the next station. Not one passenger helped the boys. The old man for whom Junaid had vacated his seat joined the others in goading the killers. At the station, no railway staff or vendor helped the boys even as the youngest among them bled to death.

For most Indians, this contrast recalled by Harsh Mander is painful beyond description. But it was early in the morning of 31 July in the year when I am writing this (2023), that an even more horrific train shooting occurred. The Jaipur-to-Mumbai Express was about 60 miles short of its destination and close to Palghar when an armed Railway Protection Force constable named Chetan Singh killed, first, a senior officer named Tika Ram Meena (who had evidently tried to restrain him) and then walked through the moving train to gun down three Muslim passengers: Abdul Kaderbhai Bhanpurwala, Sadar Mohammed Hussain and Asghar Abbas Shaikh.

The beards of the three had confirmed their Muslimness and therefore, as far as Chetan Singh was concerned, it would appear, his right to kill them. The passengers' protector had become their killer.[99]

Mercifully, there is more to India, and to India's trains, than the cruelty that in 2017 targeted Junaid and his brothers and Tika Ram Meena, Abdul Kaderbhai Bhanpurwala, Sadar Mohammed Hussain and Asghar Abbas Shaikh in 2023. In February 2023, I received the following letter from a young Madhya Pradesh lawyer, Mohan Dixit:

> Some days back, in connection with my work, I travelled from Ganj Basoda in Madhya Pradesh to Gwalior by the GT Express in an unreserved compartment. Also in that compartment were three persons, sitting together, who from their clothes and appearance seemed to be Muslims. When the train stopped at Lalitpur station, two UP police jawans entered our compartment. Ignoring the other passengers, they only questioned the three Muslims. When one of the three gave his name... the policemen asked him to produce his Aadhaar card. All three were questioned as if they were suspects. I saw tears well up in their eyes.
>
> I could not bear to see people being questioned just because of their religion. I stood up and with folded hands asked for forgiveness from the three. I told them: 'I am apologizing on behalf of the community whose members have harassed you for belonging to your religion, for I too belong to that community. My Hindu religion never taught me to frighten or intimidate anyone. My Ram teaches me to stand with the suffering, the deprived, the exploited, the weak. The Ram of whom

> Tulsidas has written wants me to be free from fear. Ram's friends were not rajas or maharajas. His friends were humiliated beings like Kevat, Sabari, Jatayu, Sugreev, Vibhishan, monkeys and bears.'
>
> Having heard what I was saying, the policemen quickly moved away from our compartment. Passengers sitting near me supported what I had said, and when, as the train reached Gwalior, I picked up my bag to leave, those Muslim fellow-passengers hugged me the way a long-separated brother would.

Mohan Dixit seems to have done what his humanity urged him to do. 'No big deal,' he would probably say about his role.

~

Before concluding this study, let us mark a crucial, and relatively recent, development: *the whole world has become the home of the Indian people.* Not only are large numbers of Indians settling in the US, Canada, the UK, Australia, Germany, France, and elsewhere, they are starting to occupy influential positions in their new homes.

Although the clash between supremacy and democracy is undoubtedly global, nations where democracy has stronger roots offer better opportunities for entering Indians to rise to higher and even topmost levels. This is true in professions such as IT, medicine, the media, engineering, management, and many more, including politics. Nations that seem to take liberty, equality and fraternity seriously are the nations where women and men of Indian origin are making conspicuous progress.

This trend carries meaning. It multiplies the importance of defending fraternity (and liberty and equality) within India.

It also raises a tremendous question. *The whole world is becoming the home of people of Indian origin, but when will India become truly accessible to all Indians?* Lucky or privileged Indians can go and live anywhere in the world, but the great majority must make do within their well-marked, confined, poor and overcrowded areas inside India.

We have to ask: will a day come when India's Dalits, Adivasis and Muslims can walk on India's lanes with heads held high, rent homes in localities they like, complete train rides without anxiety?

Fraternity within India, a solidarity that excludes no one, is more than a prerequisite for India's good name in the world. It is a condition for India's survival. Without it, 'the dignity of the individual and the unity and integrity of the nation' remains in jeopardy.

~

On the night of 28 November 2023, relief was felt across India when, one by one, all the 41 men trapped in a tunnel in Uttarakhand came out alive after seventeen days of suspense. Fraternity's noble scent also spread nationwide as we learnt the names of the twelve toilers who, after giant machines failed, had dug with their hands the hole through which the trapped men surfaced.

With her gracious permission, I quote the lines that West Bengal's young poet Moumita Alam wrote in *The Wire* about these diggers.[100]

> What are your names?
>
> Feroz, Munna Quereshi, Rashid, Irshad, Naseem,
>
> Monu, Naseer, Ankur, Jatin, Saurabh, Wakeel Hassan, Devender.
>
> And what are your titles?
>
> We are miners, sir.
>
> But what are your titles?
>
> We don't have any.
>
> We never had any.
>
> We are miners or labourers or farmers or mill workers
>
> or the thousands who die unnamed
>
> cleaning the nullahs and the sewages.
>
> We are bound by our sweat, oppression and precarity.
>
> This is our title in India, sir.

Suggested Readings

Ambedkar, B.R., *The Annihilation of Caste*, 1936 (available online: https://ccnmtl.columbia.edu/projects/mmt/ambedkar/web/readings/aoc_print_2004.pdf)

Gandhi, M.K., *Hind Swaraj*, 1909, edited by Anthony Parel, Cambridge: Cambridge University Press, 1997

___, *Constructive Programme*, Ahmedabad: Navajivan, 1945

Habib, S. Irfan, *Maulana Azad: A Life*, New Delhi: Aleph, 2023

Mander, Harsh, 'Fraternity: The Missing Link of India's Democracy', *The India Forum*, 13 February 2019 (https://www.theindiaforum.in/article/fraternity-missing-link-india-s-democracy)

Rao, B. Shiva, ed., *The Framing of India's Constitution: Select Documents*, Vol. III, New Delhi: The Indian Institute of Public Administration, 1967 (Digital Library of India Item 2015.278539)

Rogoff, Martin, 'A Comparison of Constitutionalism in France and the United States', *Maine Law Review*, vol. 49, no. 1 (1997), pp. 21–84 (available online: https://mainelaw.maine.edu/faculty/wp-content/uploads/sites/4/rogoff-mlr-49.pdf)

Endnotes

1 From B.R. Ambedkar, *Waiting for a Visa*, probably written in 1935 or 1936 (available online: http://www.columbia.edu/itc/mealac/pritchett/00ambedkar/txt_ambedkar_waiting.html, accessed on 6 December 2023).

2 In Ahmedabad, 13 April 1921. *Collected Works of Mahatma Gandhi* (hereinafter *CWMG*) (New Delhi: Publications Division), vol. 19, pp. 569–74.

3 N.K. Bose, *My Days with Gandhi* (Calcutta: Nishana, 1953), p. 8, and N.K. Bose, *Lectures on Gandhism* (Ahmedabad: Navajivan, 1971), p. 65.

4 Bose, *Lectures on Gandhism*, p. 106.

5 See D.G. Tendulkar, *Mahatma*, Vol. 7, p. 350; also *CWMG*, vol. 86, p. 305.

6 Bhadra Sinha, '"History can't haunt present"—SC dismisses plea to rename roads, places named after "invaders"', *The Print*, 27 February 2023 (https://theprint.in/judiciary/history-cant-haunt-present-sc-dismisses-plea-to-rename-roads-places-named-after-invaders/1403158/, accessed on 6 December 2023).

7 See 'Declaration of the Rights of Man–1789', available

online through The Avalon Project of the Yale Law School's Lillian Goldman Law Library (https://avalon.law.yale.edu/18th_century/rightsof.asp, accessed on 6 December 2023).

8 See Martin Rogoff, 'A Comparison of Constitutionalism in France and the United States' (available online: https://mainelaw.maine.edu/faculty/wp-content/uploads/sites/4/rogoff-mlr-49.pdf, accessed on 6 December 2023).

9 'Liberty, Equality, Fraternity', French Foreign Ministry website (https://www.diplomatie.gouv.fr/en/coming-to-france/france-facts/symbols-of-the-republic/article/liberty-equality-fraternity, accessed on 6 December 2023).

10 Ibid.

11 'Liberté, Égalité, Fraternité: The Meaning and History of France's National Motto', Civil Liberties Union for Europe website (https://www.liberties.eu/en/stories/liberte-egalite-fraternite/43532, accessed on 6 December 2023).

12 R.C. Majumdar, *Ancient India* (Delhi: Motilal Banarsidass, 1952), p. 2.

13 B.R. Ambedkar, *Writings and Speeches*, edited by Vasant Moon (Bombay: Education Department, 1979), Vol. 7, p. 26.

14 *CWMG*, vol. 76, p. 397.

15 Majumdar, *Ancient India*, p. 16.

16 Abul Kalam Azad, 'Presidential Address to the Fifty-Third Session of the Indian National Congress, Ramgarh, 1940' (available online: http://www.columbia.edu/itc/mealac/pritchett/00litlinks/txt_azad_congress_1940.html, accessed on 6 December 2023).

17 Letter from the Wood Papers cited in S.R. Mehrotra, *The Emergence of the Indian National Congress* (New Delhi: Vikas, 1971), p. 105.

18 Letter of 19 October 1939, Linlithgow Papers, India Office Library, London.

19 Quoted in Afzal Iqbal, *Mohamed Ali* (Delhi: Idarah-i-Adabiyat), pp. 379–82.

20 *CWMG*, vol. 15, p. 203.

21 In October 1939 and April and May 1940. See *CWMG*, vol. 77, p. 27; vol. 78, p. 109; and vol. 79, p. 231.

22 On 28 May 1947; *CWMG*, vol. 95, pp. 161–2.

23 *CWMG*, vol. 96, pp. 361–5.

24 Rudrangshu Mukherjee, *Tagore & Gandhi: Walking Alone, Walking Together* (New Delhi: Aleph, 2021), pp. 83–84.

25 Dhananjay Keer, *Mahatma Jotirao Phooley: Father of the Indian Social Revolution* (Bombay: Popular Prakashan, 1974), pp. 219–21.

26 M.K. Gandhi, *Hind Swaraj*, 1909, edited by Anthony Parel (Cambridge: Cambridge University Press, 1997), pp. 52–54.

27 Churchill's remark in the House of Commons on 12 March 1931, in Robert Rhodes James (ed.), *Winston Churchill: His Complete Speeches* (New York: Chelsea House, 1974), vol. V (1928–1935), p. 4995.

28 A partly speculative discussion on others who may have contributed to the text may be seen in Kama Maclean, 'The Fundamental Rights Resolution: Nationalism, Internationalism and Cosmopolitanism in an Interwar

Moment', *Comparative Studies of South Asia, Africa and the Middle East*, vol. 37, no 2 (2017) (https://doi.org/10.1215/1089201x-4132833).

29 *CWMG*, vol. 45, pp. 370–74.
30 Ibid., vol. 47, p. 247.
31 Ibid., vol. 48, p. 258.
32 Ibid., p. 298.
33 Mahadev Desai, *The Diary of Mahadev Desai* (Ahmedabad: Navajivan, 1953); see also *CWMG*, vol. 51, p. 62.
34 *CWMG*, vol. 51, p. 55.
35 Ibid., p. 119.
36 Pyarelal, *The Epic Fast* (Ahmedabad, 1932), p. 59.
37 Ibid., pp. 89 and 93.
38 *CWMG*, vol. 51, p. 139.
39 B.R. Ambedkar, *What Congress and Gandhi Have Done to the Untouchables* (1945), p. 103.
40 Pyarelal, *The Epic Fast*, p. 59.
41 Ambedkar, *What Congress and Gandhi Have Done to the Untouchables*, pp. 90–91.
42 Ibid., p. 259.
43 On 26 September 1932; CWMG, vol. 51, p. 144.
44 Ibid., p. 144.
45 Ibid., p. 154.
46 On 5 November 1932; ibid., p. 347.
47 The government's reprisals forced the closure of *Navajivan* and its English-language counterpart, *Young India*.
48 *CWMG*, vol. 55, pp. 53–54.
49 *CWMG*, vol. 53, p. 306.
50 Desai, *The Diary of Mahadev Desai*, Vol. 1.

51 *CWMG*, vol. 53, pp. 13–24.
52 Ibid., pp. 309–10.
53 Ibid., vol. 55, p. 74.
54 Ibid., pp. 196–99.
55 Andrews's letter quoted in David M. Gracie (ed.), *Gandhi & Charlie* (Cambridge, Mass.: Cowley, 1989), p. 155.
56 *CWMG*, vol. 55, pp. 198–99.
57 Ibid., vol. 57, p. 27.
58 Ibid., pp. 44–46.
59 Ibid., pp. 503–4.
60 Ibid., p. 47.
61 Ibid., p. 304.
62 Ibid., pp. 458–59.
63 *CWMG*, vol. 58, p. 102.
64 On 16 June 1934; ibid., p. 82.
65 On 10 July 1934; ibid., p. 166.
66 A timeline of Ambedkar's life is provided on the website maintained by Prof Emerita Frances W. Pritchett, Columbia University (http://www.columbia.edu/itc/mealac/pritchett/00ambedkar/timeline/1930s.html, accessed on 6 December 2023).
67 See B.R. Ambedkar, *Untouchables or The Children of India's Ghetto!* (1935), Part II (available online: https://www.roundtableindia.co.in/untouchables-or-the-children-of-indias-ghetto-part-ii-32662/, accessed on 6 December 2023).
68 See timeline of Ambedkar's life on the website maintained by F.W. Pritchett, citing Dhananjay Keer, *Dr Ambedkar: Life and Mission* (Bombay: Popular Prakashan, 1971

[1954]), p. 253 (http://www.columbia.edu/itc/mealac/pritchett/00ambedkar/timeline/1930s.html, accessed on 6 December 2023).

69 'B.R. Ambedkar: Yeola Declaration on Caste and Conversion', Berkley Center for Religion, Peace and World Affairs website (https://berkleycenter.georgetown.edu/quotes/b-r-ambedkar-yeola-declaration-on-caste-and-conversion, accessed on 6 December 2023).

70 *CWMG*, vol. 62, p. 37.

71 See Dr Ambedkar's views on Gandhi's reaction. 'How Gandhi Reacted to Dr Ambedkar's Decision to Leave Hinduism at Yeola', Velivada (website), citing B.R. Ambedkar's *Writings and Speeches*, Vol. 17 (Part III) (https://velivada.com/2017/05/14/how-gandhi-reacted-to-dr-ambedkars-decision-to-leave-hinduism-at-yeola/, accessed on 6 December 2023).

72 *CWMG*, vol. 62, p. 121.

73 Ibid., 142.

74 See *The Annihilation of Caste* (available online: https://ccnmtl.columbia.edu/projects/mmt/ambedkar/web/index.html, accessed on 6 December 2023).

75 In the second edition, published in 1945, of *Pakistan or the Partition of India*, Ambedkar wrote: 'Mr Gandhi and Mr Jinnah in their recent talks cited the book as an authority on the subject which might be consulted with advantage...' (The book is available online: https://franpritchett.com/00ambedkar/ambedkar_partition/index.html#contents, accessed on 6 December 2023).

76 See Chapter XIII, 'Must There Be Pakistan?', *Pakistan or the Partition of India*.

77 On 3 February 1947. *CWMG*, vol. 86, p. 426.

78 M.S. Gore, *The Social Context of an Ideology* (New Delhi: Sage, 1993), pp. 180–81. Gore cites, in translation, from Changdeo Bhavanrao Khairmode's 12-volume Marathi biography of Ambedkar. Khairmode (1904–1971) was one of Ambedkar's close friends and earliest biographers.

79 *Constituent Assembly Debates*, 25 November 1949 (see https://indiankanoon.org/doc/792941/, accessed on 6 December 2023).

80 See p. 510 of *The Framing of India's Constitution: Select Documents*, Vol. III, edited by B. Shiva Rao (Digital Library of India Item 2015.278539).

81 *Constituent Assembly Debates*, 25 November 1949.

82 M.K. Gandhi, in chapter titled 'Adivasi', *Constructive Programme* (Ahmedabad: Navajivan, 1945), new edition, p. 24.

83 Claudio Corradetti writes in this connection of the philosopher Axel Honneth and the political sociologist Hauke Brunkhorst, both from Germany (https://iep.utm.edu/critical-theory-frankfurt-school/, accessed on 6 December 2023). My gratitude to Neera Chandhoke for hints regarding the Frankfurt School and the Balkans.

84 Harsh Mander, 'Fraternity: The Missing Link of India's Democracy', *The India Forum*, 13 February 2019 (https://www.theindiaforum.in/article/fraternity-missing-link-india-s-democracy, accessed on 6 December 2023).

85 *CWMG*, vol. 89, p. 461.

86 Abul Kalam Azad, 'Presidential Address to the Fifty-Third Session of the Indian National Congress, Ramgarh, 1940'.

87 Subhashini Ali, 'The Sangh's Attempts to Appropriate the Secular Netaji Will Simply Not Work', *The Wire*, 22 September 2022 (https://thewire.in/politics/sangh-cannot-appropriate-netaji-subhas-chandra-bose-secularism, accessed on 6 December 2023).

88 I should acknowledge Hilal Ahmed's reminders to me of the roles of Leftists and Progressives.

89 *India After 1947: Reflections & Recollections* (New Delhi: Aleph, 2022).

90 'Following Akhand Bharat mural in new Parliament, Kathmandu mayor installs map of "Greater Nepal"', *The Telegraph*, 10 June 2023 (https://www.telegraphindia.com/india/following-akhand-bharat-mural-in-new-parliament-kathmandu-mayor-installs-map-of-greater-nepal/cid/1943888, accessed on 6 December 2023).

91 *CWMG*, vol. 75, p. 147.

92 B.R. Ambedkar, 'Why Was Nagpur Chosen?', first published in Marathi in *Prabudh Bharat* ('Enlightened India'), 27 October 1956, translated by Rekha Damle and Eleanor Zelliot, August–September 1964 (available online: http://www.columbia.edu/itc/mealac/pritchett/00ambedkar/txt_ambedkar_conversion.html, accessed on 6 December 2023).

93 *We, or Our Nationhood Defined*, pp. 77–78.

94 Ibid., p. 88.

95 Ibid., p. 93.

96 Harsh Mander, 'Fraternity: The Missing Link of India's Democracy', *The India Forum*.

97 'Mom of Portland train hero Taliesin Meche says her son "had a lot of bravery in his spirit"', *The Seattle Times*,

30 May 2017 (https://www.seattletimes.com/seattle-news/law-justice/mom-of-taliesin-meche-says-portland-train-victim-known-for-brave-spirit, accessed on 6 December 2023).

98 'Teen on Portland train: "They lost their lives because of me and my friend"', CNN, 30 May 2017 (https://www.cnn.com/2017/05/29/us/portland-train-teenager-stabbing/index.html, accessed on 6 December 2023).

99 'RPF Constable Kills Officer, Three Muslim Passengers in Hate Crime Onboard Running Train', *The Wire*, 1 August 2020. *The Wire*'s report of the killings includes quotes from the *Hindustan Times* and *The Indian Express* (https://thewire.in/security/railway-protection-force-constable-shoots-dead-asi-three-others-in-train, accessed on 6 December 2023).

100 'What Are Your Names?' was published on *LiveWire* on 1 December 2023. See Moumita Alam, 'The Light That Peeps in Through the Holes: Two Poems on Rat-Hole Miners' (https://livewire.thewire.in/livewire/the-light-that-peeps-in-through-the-holes-two-poems-on-rat-hole-miners/, accessed on 11 December 2023.)